EDUCAT

in the UK

Facts & Figures

THIRD EDITION

EDUCATION
in the UK
Facts & Figures
THIRD EDITION

Donald Mackinnon
June Statham

Hodder & Stoughton
in association with

The Open University

A catalogue record for this title is available from the British Library

ISBN 0340 73029 3

First edition published 1995
Second edition published 1996
Third edition published 1999
Impression number   10 9 8 7 6 5 4 3
Year   2004   2003 2002

Typeset by Wearset, Boldon, Tyne and Wear.
Printed in Great Britain for Hodder & Stoughton Educational, a division of Hodder Headline Plc,
338 Euston Road, London NW1 3BH by The Bath Press, Bath

CONTENTS

Education in the United Kingdom: Facts and Figures has been written in the first instance as a set book for the Open University course EU208, *Exploring Educational Issues*. But it has been designed to stand independently of the course, and we hope it will also be found useful by people studying other courses, in the Open University or elsewhere, and by anyone interested in education, whether as a parent, teacher, student or citizen.

This book has grown out of a previous one by the same authors, *The Education Fact File*, but it has been extensively rewritten and revised throughout. As we have to emphasise again and again in the chapters that follow, we are living in a period of rapid and profound change in education, beginning but certainly not ending with the Education Reform Act of 1988. Like its predecessor, the present book will inevitably become outdated in its turn, and the authors and publishers hope to produce new, up-to-date editions as the need arises. Accordingly, we would welcome any comments, criticisms, suggestions for inclusion, and above all corrections of any mistakes or misunderstandings.

This is not a work of original research. Almost all our information comes from published sources, mainly official publications but also academic research and other reference books more specialised than this one. For this edition, we have also made use of some of the government's websites (see the list at the end of this chapter). These sources are acknowledged at the end of each chapter. (If any source we have used has inadvertently been omitted, we apologise, and ask to be told so that proper acknowledgement can be made in subsequent editions.) Our contribution has been to try to select the most significant information from those sources, and to present it in as clear and informative a manner as we can, in words and diagrams.

In preparing the book and its predecessors, we have received a great deal of assistance from many people and institutions, and we cannot acknowledge them all individually. We are extremely grateful nonetheless. Particular thanks are due to Geoffrey Walford, Bob Morris, Dominic Newbould, Lorna Unwin, Martin Watkinson, Mary James, Will Swann and the staff of the Open University Library. We have been able to follow most though not all of their suggestions, and of course the responsibility for omissions and any remaining mistakes is ours.

NOTE TO THE THIRD EDITION

The first edition of this book was published in 1995, and just four years later, there have been changes to the education system important enough to require two further editions. We have tried to bring the book fully up to date as we go to press in early 1999, both in our descriptions of educational structures and processes and in our statistics. We hope we have not overlooked any important changes, but these have been so many and so rapid that we can never be completely sure. As before, we welcome any corrections, criticisms or suggestions from our readers. We are very grateful to those who drew our attention to mistakes and outdated material in our last edition.

Anyone who compares our figures here with those of the previous editions will discover that we have not always updated them in exactly the same form. Occasionally we have not updated them at all. This is usually because the official sources on which we depend for most of our information often change the ways in which they collect and present information, for reasons not always self-evident.

OFFICIAL WEBSITES

DfEE: http//www.dfee.gov.uk
OFSTED: http//www.ofsted.gov.uk
Scottish Office: http//www.scotland.gov.uk
Welsh Office: http//www.wales.gov.uk
DENI: http//www.nics.gov.uk/deni/index.htm

Education in the UK: Facts and Figures aims to provide basic factual informa-tion, in words, diagrams and numbers, about education in the United Kingdom today.

In Section One, we present some information about the social and histori-cal background to current events and issues. Chapter 2 gives an outline of some social structures and processes that are important for education. Chapter 3 summarises the principal official reports on education and related subjects that have been prepared since the Education Act of 1944. And Chapter 4 outlines the most important educational legislation from the Education Act of 1870 to those of 1998.

In Section Two, we describe the educational systems of the four countries that make up the United Kingdom. The principal educational institutions are outlined in Chapter 5; the ways in which they are organised and controlled are explained in Chapter 6. Chapter 7 looks at the educational professionals who work in various ways within the systems. Chapter 8 outlines the procedures of educational finance and resources – where the money comes from, and where it goes. Finally, Chapter 9 summarises the main qualifications available at every level within (and outside) the education systems.

Section Three covers a variety of processes occurring within these educa-tion systems. Chapter 10 looks at the school curriculum and its assessment after the 1988 Education Reform Act. Chapter 11 provides information about a set of issues that have long been at the centre of educational debate and controversy – educational attainment, and its relationship to equality and inequality between children from different groups and categories. And Chapter 12 summarises the position today of young people just over school-leaving age: the new problems they face, the new possibilities open to them.

Section Four has just two chapters, both in the form of alphabetical lists: Chapter 13 is a glossary of important educational terms, and Chapter 14 deciphers some of the most widespread educational acronyms and abbrevia-tions that are treated more fully in other chapters, as well as some that are not covered elsewhere in the book.

FACTS AND FIGURES

All these chapters are intended to be *factual*, to tell the reader what the educa-tional world is like, not to give the interpretation or judgements – and cer-tainly not the prejudices – of the authors or anyone else. This is a worthwhile aim, we believe, but one impossible to fulfil. Although we have done our best to fulfil it, we must offer some words of caution about taking the contents of this book as facts, let alone *the* facts about education.

First, and most obviously, the book is bound to contain errors. Some of these may come from our sources; others, alas, will be all our own work. We hope that these are few and trivial, and we deeply regret every one of them, but it is inevitable that a book of this character will have some.

Second, we have inevitably made choices about which facts to include, and which to leave out. Sometimes these have been slightly forced choices, because of gaps and limitations in the available data. But much more often, we have had to decide what we considered most significant and telling from an embarrassment of information. This is where interpretation is unavoidable, and prejudice a very real danger. We cannot, of course, claim to be unprejudiced; people are not normally aware of their own prejudices. What we can and do say is that we have never knowingly excluded or modified any information in order to favour our own beliefs, values or political preferences.

Third, even the categories in which data are presented depend on controversial judgements, and are open to unintended distortion. There are different ways of defining 'social class', for example, or of identifying ethnic groups, and these can lead to very different pictures of the class structure or ethnic composition of the country, and of the relationship between class or ethnicity and, say, educational attainment. The particular cases of social class and ethnic group are discussed in Chapter 11; here we want to make the general point that choosing categories for presenting 'the facts' is fraught with uncertainty and controversy.

Finally, we would like to warn against leaping too quickly to what may seem obvious interpretations of facts and their relationships, such as conclusions about cause and effect. Above all, we should be cautious about accepting plausible interpretations of one fact or set of facts in isolation, without at least checking that our interpretation fits in with other relevant information.

READING AND REFERRING

One of the first things we had to decide in preparing this book was whether it was to be primarily a reference book, to be consulted as required for some particular piece of information, or a genuine text, to be read through from beginning to end. As you will see, it has ended up as something of both. Four of the chapters are really elaborated lists: Chapters 3 and 4 present their reports and Acts in chronological order; Chapters 13 and 14 list their terms and acronyms in alphabetical order. We do not expect many people to read their way through these chapters; on the other hand, if you want to look up the main provisions of, say, the 1987 Teachers' Pay and Conditions Act, or distinguish GIST from GEST, you will find the information easily accessible there.

The other chapters, though, *are* designed to be read through as well as referred to. They deal with subject matter that does not so readily lend itself to division into self-contained entries. We hope that each chapter provides a clear and straightforward introduction to the basic facts and figures in the area it covers. The inevitable disadvantage is that it is not quite so easy to look things up in these chapters as it would be in a list. Besides, many topics do not fit neatly into one, and only one, chapter or section, however carefully these are devised. But the book has a comprehensive index, and cross-references within and between chapters. With judicious use of these, we hope, you should not have great difficulty in finding out what you want to know.

SCOPE

The book covers the whole of the United Kingdom – England, Scotland, Wales (which together form Great Britain) and Northern Ireland. (It does not cover the Isle of Man or the Channel Islands; they are not part of the United Kingdom, but Crown dependencies, with their own governments.) However, its coverage of these countries is far from equal. England, or for some purposes England and Wales together, receives the most attention. Whether this is justified is open to argument; we are far from certain that we have always got the balance right. England is, of course, by far the biggest country in the United Kingdom, with 84% of its population (England and Wales together have 88%) (see Chapter 2, Figure 2.1). By virtue of its size, developments in English education have usually exerted greater influence on the other countries than theirs on England. And a practical point: published data on English education are usually more extensive and detailed. We have tried to use United Kingdom data whenever we could, but often we have had to illustrate particular points from English, or English and Welsh, figures. We hope this does not mislead; we always try to make clear what countries or regions our figures cover.

Of course there are differences between the countries in the structure of their education systems, and in the processes within them, and these are likely to increase after devolution takes effect from the middle of 1999. But even before devolution, Northern Ireland, for example, still has its grammar schools, whereas maintained schools in England, Scotland and Wales are now almost entirely comprehensive. Scotland has its own system of school examinations and vocational qualifications; England, Wales and Northern Ireland share a common system. And so on. Differences in structure are spelled out in the appropriate chapters, and where we judge there to be significant differences in educational processes from country to country, we have pointed them out.

CHANGE

Finally, we are only too well aware that we have produced this book during what promises to be a period of the most profound, widespread and rapid educational change for many years – beginning, but certainly not ending with the 1988 Education Reform Act. In almost every chapter, we have had to point forward to what seem to be the likeliest important developments in the near future, as well as describing things as they are now.

NOTE TO THE READER

In the references and bibliographies, the following abbreviations are used:

ACAC	Awdurdod Cwricwlwm ac Asesu Cymru (Curriculum and Assessment Authority for Wales)
CIPFA	Chartered Institute of Public Finance and Accountancy
COI	Central Office of Information
CRAC	Careers Research and Advisory Centre
CSO	Central Statistical Office
DENI	Department of Education Northern Ireland
DES	Department of Education and Science
DETR	Department of Environment, Transport and Regions
DFE	Department for Education
DfEE	Department for Education and Employment
EDG	Employment Department Group
GSS	Government Statistical Service
HEFC	Higher Education Funding Council
HESA	Higher Education Statistics Agency
HMSO	Her Majesty's Stationery Office
ISIS	Independent Schools Information Service
NCC	National Curriculum Council
NFER	National Foundation for Educational Research
NISRA	Northern Ireland Statistics and Research Agency
OFSTED	Office for Standards in Education
OHMCI	Office of Her Majesty's Chief Inspector of Schools (in Wales)
ONS	Office for National Statistics
OPCS	Office of Population Censuses and Surveys
SCAA	School Curriculum and Assessment Authority
SED	Scottish Education Department
SOED	Scottish Office Education Department
SOEID	Scottish Office Education and Industry Department

Numbers in this book are usually 'rounded'; occasionally this means that percentages add up to slightly more or less than 100. Dates are usually given as they appear in the sources. Where two years are mentioned (e.g. 1996–7), this refers to a single academic year (or, where appropriate, a single financial year). It does not mean the two calendar years (1996 and 1997). Where a single year is mentioned (e.g. 1996), this usually refers to the point in the calendar year when the information was collected.

Social factors of fundamental importance for the education system include the size of the population, its structure by age and sex, its distribution across nations and regions, its composition by social class and ethnic group and – not least – the ways in which any of these change from year to year.

POPULATION

The United Kingdom has a total population of 58.8 million, divided unevenly among its four constituent countries as shown in Figure 2.1.

Since 1994, England has been divided into 10 *Government Office Regions* (GOR), which are now used in official statistics instead of the eight standard statistical regions previously used. Their populations are shown in Figure 2.2. (For an explanation of the relationship between the old and the new regions, see ONS, 1997b, Introduction and Chapter 1.)

Figure 2.3 gives, for Great Britain, the numbers of males and females in each of five age groups below the age of 25. These are the people most likely to be, now or in the very near future, full-time pupils or students in educational institutions.

The size of the population of school or college age has important implications for educational policy and planning. It affects the number of schools (see

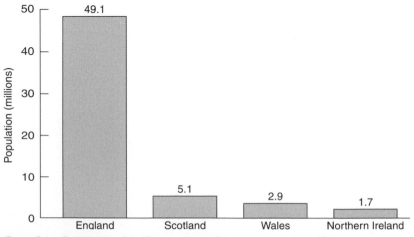

Figure 2.1   Populations of the four countries of the United Kingdom, 1996 (Adapted from ONS, 1998b, Tables 2.1 and 2.2)

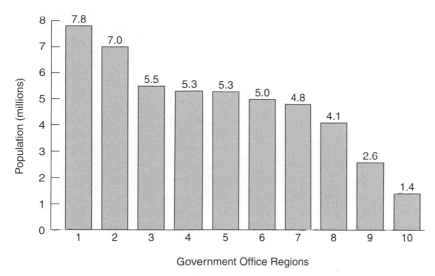

Figure 2.2   Populations of the ten Government Office Regions of England, 1995
(Adapted from ONS, 1997b, Table 3.10)
Key to regions: 1 South East; 2 London; 3 North West; 4 West Midlands; 5 Eastern;
6 Yorkshire and the Humber; 7 South West; 8 East Midlands; 9 North East; 10 Merseyside

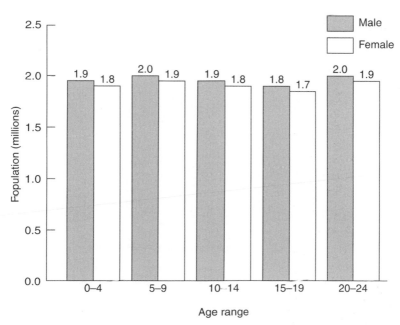

Figure 2.3   The under-25 population of the United Kingdom by age and sex, 1996
(Adapted from ONS, 1998b, Table 2.2)

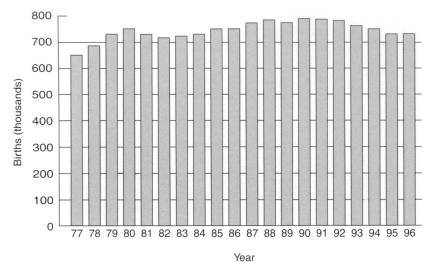

Figure 2.4   Births in the United Kingdom, 1977–96
(Adapted from CSO, 1982, Table 2.24; CSO, 1994, Table 2.16; ONS, 1998a, Table 2.14)

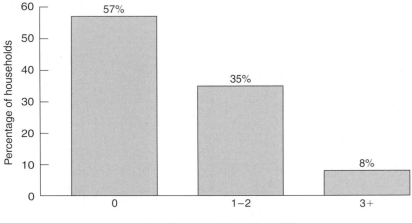

Figure 2.5   Percentages of one-family, married or cohabiting couple households with
various numbers of dependent children aged under 18, Great Britain, 1996–7
(Adapted from ONS, 1998c, Table 2.3)

Chapter 5) and the number of teachers (see Chapter 7) required, and therefore affects the amount of expenditure needed by the education system (see Chapter 8). Changes from year to year in the number of people in each age group create difficulties for planning, especially as birth rates are notoriously difficult to predict; estimating what the school population will be in more than five years' time becomes increasingly speculative and uncertain. Figure 2.4 shows how the number of births in the United Kingdom has varied from year to year since 1977, when it reached its lowest post-war figure.

The population of Great Britain grew steadily from the end of World War II until the early 1970s (an increase of roughly 5% per decade), since when it has grown more slowly (about 1% per decade). But the *age structure* within this total has changed in the same period towards fewer younger and more older people. In 1996, 19% of the population were under 15 (compared with 24% in 1971), and 16% were 65 or over (compared with 13% in 1971) (ONS, 1998a, Table 2.3).

HOUSEHOLD AND FAMILY

A third of all households in Great Britain had, in 1996, at least one dependent child. Of these children, 79% lived with an adult couple, and 22% with a lone parent (20% with a mother, 2% with a father) (ONS, 1998d, Table 2.4).

The majority of families are small. The average number of dependent children in all families with dependent children in 1996 was 1.8 (but see Figure 2.14 below). The distribution of family sizes among married or cohabiting couples in 1996–7 is shown in Figure 2.5.

Since World War II, births outside marriage have increased sevenfold as a percentage of all births in the United Kingdom, from 5% (1951) to 35% (1996). During the same period, divorces have also increased: in England and Wales the increase was more than fourfold, from 0.3% to 1.3% of the married population per annum (ONS, 1997b, Tables 2.12 and 2.15).

Men are more likely than women to be 'economically active', that is, to be in or seeking paid employment (see Figure 2.8), but this difference is decreasing with time (see Figure 2.9). Women with dependent children are less likely to have full-time jobs, but more likely to have part-time jobs, than women without. The younger her youngest child is, the less likely a mother is to have any employment, full- or part-time, as Figure 2.6 shows.

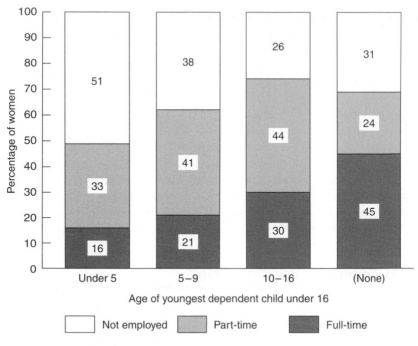

Figure 2.6   *Percentages of women in employment, by age of youngest dependent child under 16, Great Britain, 1996*
(Adapted from ONS, 1997a, Table A15)

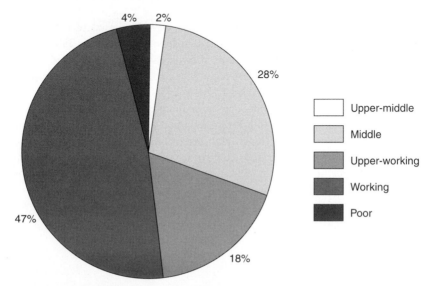

Figure 2.7   *Self-rated social class, Great Britain, 1991*
(Adapted from Jowell et al. (eds) 1992, p. 177)

SOCIAL CLASS AND OCCUPATION

The terms 'working class' and 'middle class' are in widespread use, but under many different definitions and interpretations, which can lead to different pictures of the class structure of the country. One way of obtaining figures for the classes is to ask people what class they think they belong to. When asked their social class, about 65% of people in Great Britain identify themselves as working (or 'upper working') class, and about 30% as middle (or 'upper middle') class. (Slightly more identify their parents as working class, and fewer identify their parents as middle class.) Figure 2.7 gives more detail about 'self-rated' social class.

But demographers and social scientists also use more objective measures. The most common practice in educational research is to take *occupation* as the basis for identifying class, often adopting one of the official classifications of

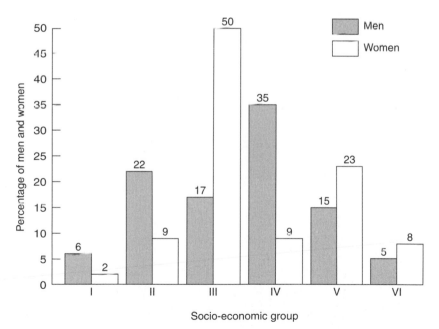

Figure 2.8   *Percentages of men and of women in each socioeconomic group, Great Britain 1996*

Key: I Professional; II Employers and managers; III Intermediate and junior non-manual; IV Skilled manual and self-employed non-professional; V Semi-skilled manual and personal service; VI Unskilled manual

(Adapted from ONS, 1998d, Table 5.6)

occupations used by the Office of National Statistics (ONS), for example *socioeconomic groups*:

1 Professional
2 Employers and managers
3 Intermediate and junior non-manual
4 Skilled manual and self-employed non-professional
5 Semi-skilled manual and personal service
6 Unskilled manual

Figure 2.8 shows the percentages of men and of women in Great Britain in 1996 in these socioeconomic groups.

In practice, most educational researchers studying social class have used simplified or compressed versions of the ONS classifications. Frequently, groups 1–3 are taken to be middle class, and 4–6 to be working class. Children are generally classified according to their fathers' occupations.

Substantially more men than women are economically active. However, differences between the sexes in economic activity have diminished over the years. This is illustrated in Figure 2.9.

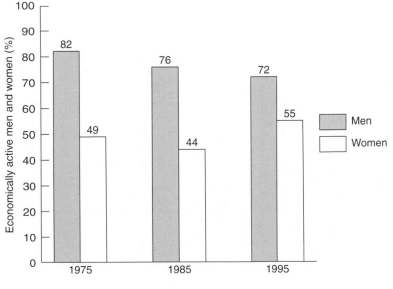

Figure 2.9   Percentages of men and women over 16 who are economically active, Great Britain, 1975–95
(Adapted from ONS, 1998d, Table 5.10)

Women in employment are more likely than men to be employed part-time: 50% of married women and 38% of unmarried women in 1996, compared with 8% of men (ONS, 1998d, Table 5.18. Official statistics do not distinguish between married and unmarried men here).

In recent decades, the proportion of 'middle-class' people (that is, people in non-manual occupations) in the population has risen steadily, whilst that of 'working-class' people (in manual occupations) has fallen. This is illustrated in Figure 2.10 for the Census years of 1971, 1981 and 1991, using another of the ONS classifications: *social class based on occupation*.

ETHNIC GROUPS

The 1991 Census was the first to have a question on ethnic group membership. The ethnic categories used on the Census form, adopted after extensive consultation and pilot-testing (see White, 1990), were: White, Black Caribbean, Black African, Black Other, Indian, Pakistani, Bangladeshi, Chinese and Other. According to the Census, the majority ethnic group (White) had 51.9 million members in Great Britain in 1991, of whom 49.7 million were

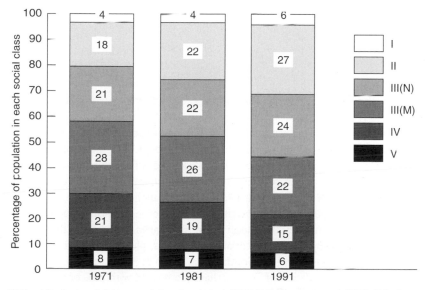

KEY: I Professional; II Managerial and technical; III(N) Skilled non-manual; III(M) Skilled manual; IV Partly skilled; V Unskilled

Figure 2.10   Social class composition of the population of Great Britain, 1971–91 (Adapted from OPCS, 1975, Table 29; OPCS, 1984, Table 16A; OPCS, 1992b, Table 6.13)

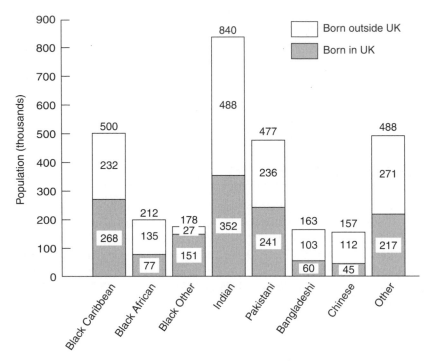

*Figure 2.11   Minority ethnic groups in Great Britain, 1991 Census
(Adapted from Teague, 1993)*

born in the United Kingdom. The numbers for each minority ethnic group are shown in Figure 2.11.

According to the Census, 94.5% of the population of Great Britain are White, while 5.5% belong to minority ethnic groups. The latter are concentrated in particular areas of the country. Two-thirds of all members of minority ethnic groups live in the former metropolitan counties of Greater London, West Midlands, West Yorkshire and Greater Manchester (compared with a quarter of the population as a whole); 45% of the ethnic minority population of Great Britain live in Greater London alone (compared with 12% of the population as a whole). By contrast, Scotland and Wales, plus the English regions of the North, East Anglia and the South West, taken together, contain 8% of the ethnic minority population of Great Britain (compared with 32% of the population as a whole) (OPCS, 1993c, Table 6).

This distribution leads to a very different ethnic composition of the population in different areas of the country. For example, 45% of the population of the London Borough of Brent belong to ethnic minority groups,

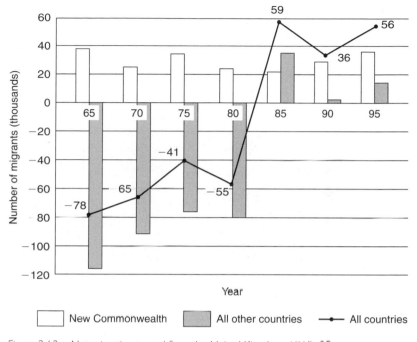

*Figure 2.12   Net migration to and from the United Kingdom, 1965–95
(Adapted from Bulusu, 1986, Table 1; Rosenbaum and Homsey, 1992, Tables 1 and 2;
ONS, 1998a, Table 2.8)*

as do 42% of the London Borough of Ealing, 29% of Leicester and 28% of
Slough. By contrast, fewer than 0.2% of the population of the Isles of Scilly or
the counties of Berwickshire or Sutherland belong to a minority ethnic group
(Teague, 1993, Table 2).

Only a minority of immigrants to the United Kingdom have come from the
New Commonwealth, and this minority has decreased in absolute terms, and
even more in proportional terms, since the mid-1960s. (Pakistan is included in
the New Commonwealth statistics throughout, even though it was not actually
a member of the Commonwealth for part of the period covered.)

In 1965, there were about 206,000 immigrants to the United Kingdom, of
whom 78,000 (38%) were from the New Commonwealth. In 1975, the total
was 197,000, and the New Commonwealth figure was 66,000 (34%). By 1995,
the total immigration figure had risen to 245,000, and the figure for the New
Commonwealth had fallen to 33,000 (13%).

Until the 1980s, there was more emigration from the United Kingdom than

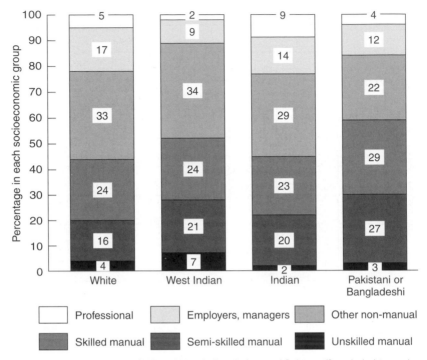

Figure 2.13   Percentages of White, West Indian, Indian and Pakistani/Bangladeshi people in each socioeconomic group, Great Britain 1989–91 (Adapted from OPCS, 1992b, Table 6.35)

immigration to it. Thus in 1965, there were about 284,000 emigrants (compared with 206,000 immigrants), and in 1975 there were 238,000 emigrants (compared with 197,000 immigrants). However, in 1983, this pattern was reversed, and the number of people leaving the United Kingdom fell below the number entering – a pattern which has persisted in most subsequent years. In 1995, there were 192,000 emigrants (compared with 245,000 immigrants) (Bulusu, 1986, Table 1; Rosenbaum and Hornsey, 1992, Tables 1 and 2; ONS, 1998a, Table 2.8).

The overall picture of migration to and from the United Kingdom from 1965 to 1990 is summarised in Figure 2.12: net immigration is shown as 'positive' migration (above the horizontal axis), and net emigration as 'negative' migration (below the axis).

With the passage of time, an increasing proportion of the ethnic minority population consists of people born in Great Britain. For example, the propor-

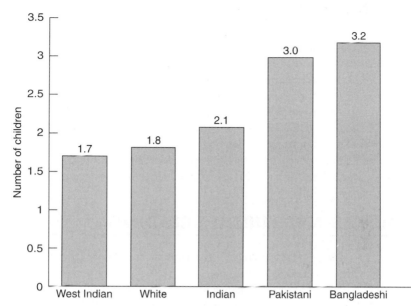

Figure 2.14 Average number of children per family in each ethnic group, Great Britain, 1987–9
(Adapted from Haskey, 1991)

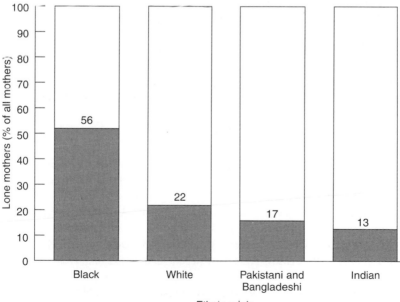

Figure 2.15 Lone parents as percentages of all families with dependent children, by ethnic group, Great Britain, 1996
(Adapted from ONS, 1998c, Table 2.11)

tion of people of Indian, Pakistani or Bangladeshi descent living in Britain who were born in Britain rose from 38% in 1985–7 to 44% in 1991. For people of Afro-Caribbean descent, the proportion also rose, though more slowly: from 52% to 53% in the same period (Haskey, 1988; Teague, 1993).

The ethnic minority population is young; in the early 1990s, 39% were aged under 20 and 6% aged 60 or over (compared with 26% under 20 and 20% aged 60 or over in the population as a whole) (ONS, 1998a, Table 2.6).

As well as age differences, ethnic groups show differences in their occupational structure (see Figure 2.13) and family patterns (see Figures 2.14 and 2.15).

SOURCES AND FURTHER READING

Bulusu, L. (1986) Recent patterns of migration from and to the United Kingdom, *Population Trends*, No. 46.

CSO (1982) *Annual Abstract of Statistics*, No. 118, London: HMSO.

CSO (1994) *Annual Abstract of Statistics*, No. 130, London: HMSO.

Haskey, J. (1988) The ethnic minority populations of Great Britain: their size and characteristics, *Population Trends*, No. 54.

Haskey, J. (1991) Estimated numbers and demographic characteristics of one-parent families in Great Britain, *Population Trends*, No. 65.

Jowell, R. et al. (eds) (1992) *British Social Attitudes: 9th Report*, Aldershot: Dartmouth.

ONS (1997a) *Living in Britain: preliminary results from the 1996 General Household Survey*, London: The Stationery Office.

ONS (1997b) *Regional Trends 32: 1997 edition*, London: The Stationery Office.

ONS (1998a) *Annual Abstract of Statistics: 1998 edition* No. 134, London: The Stationery Office.

ONS (1998b) *Monthly Digest of Statistics: June 1998*, London: The Stationery Office.

ONS (1998c) *Social Trends 28: 1998 edition*, London: The Stationery Office.

ONS (1998d) *Living in Britain: results from the 1996 General Household Survey*, London: The Stationery Office.

OPCS (1975) *Census 1971: Great Britain: Economic Activity Part IV*, London: HMSO.

OPCS (1984) *Census 1981: Economic Activity: Great Britain*, London: HMSO.

OPCS (1991) *1991 Census: Preliminary Report for England and Wales*, London: HMSO.

OPCS (1992a) *1991 Census: Definitions: Great Britain*, London: HMSO.

OPCS (1992b) *Labour Force Survey 1990 and 1991*, London: HMSO.

OPCS (1993a) *1991 Census: Sex, Age and Marital Status: Great Britain*, London: HMSO.

OPCS (1993b) *1991 Census: Historical Tables: Great Britain*, London: HMSO.

OPCS (1993c) *1991 Census: Report for Great Britain (Part 1) Volume 1*, London: HMSO.

OPCS (1994) *General Household Survey 1992*, London: HMSO.

Rosenbaum, M. and Hornsey, D. (1992) International migration 1991, *Population Trends*, No. 70.

Teague, A. (1993) Ethnic group: first results from the 1991 Census, *Population Trends*, No. 72.

White, P. (1990) A question on ethnic group for the census: findings from the 1989 test, *Population Trends*, No. 59.

This chapter contains summaries of the principal findings and recommendations of some of the major official reports on education and related topics from 1944 until the present day. Inevitably, not all reports can be covered, and the summaries of those included are brief and highly selective. (See the 'Sources and further reading' section at the end of this chapter.)

Almost all of these reports were prepared by committees of inquiry appointed directly by government ministers (though we have also included a small number of particularly important reports produced by working parties or study groups attached to government ministries). All recent committees of inquiry, and some in the past, have been set up specifically for the task in hand, but between 1944 and 1967 many of the inquiries were undertaken by the Central Advisory Councils for Education (CACE) for England and for Wales, bodies set up under the 1944 Education Act to advise ministers on important education issues. The reports are usually best known by the name of the committee's chairperson – 'The Plowden Report', 'The Warnock Report' and so on.

Where reports have led to legislation (see also Chapter 4), or were otherwise very influential, we have indicated this, with brief comments in square brackets. In some cases, though, reports seem to have had little impact, and in many others their effects are difficult to assess.

Unless otherwise indicated, the reports apply to England and Wales.

1944 FLEMING – PUBLIC SCHOOLS AND THE GENERAL EDUCATION SYSTEM

The Fleming committee was set up to consider how public schools (defined as those belonging to the Headmasters' Conference or the Governing Bodies Association, together with 'comparable schools for girls') could develop and extend their association with the general education system. The report recommended that public schools should progressively be integrated into the state system by taking pupils who would be given state grants. To begin with, it was suggested, they should allocate a quarter of their places to this scheme, but eventually all their places should be open to pupils with state grants. [Though well received by the public schools, the scheme never came into effect, mainly because of the unwillingness of either central government or LEAs to take responsibility for payment of the grants.]

1944 MCNAIR – TEACHERS AND YOUTH LEADERS

This report was concerned with the supply, recruitment and training of teachers (and youth leaders). It recommended (for both) increases in salary, and the extension of training courses to three years' full-time study.

1945 PERCY – HIGHER TECHNOLOGICAL EDUCATION

This report investigated the needs of higher technological education in England and Wales, and the role of universities and technical colleges in meeting them. It recommended expansion of universities' science teaching and the creation of colleges of advanced technology. In addition, it recommended the establishment of organisations to coordinate the work of universities, colleges of technology and technical colleges at both local and national levels.

1946 BARLOW – SCIENTIFIC MANPOWER (Cmd. 6824)

This report argued that more university places were needed, especially for science students. [More places were provided.]

1947 CLARKE – SCHOOL AND LIFE (CACE England)

This was the first CACE report. It examined 'the transition from school to independent life'. The committee interpreted its brief very widely, embracing all levels of education. Greatly increased expenditure was called for, particularly to reduce pupil/teacher ratios and improve unhealthy and unsuitable school buildings. Recommendations were made about a wide range of topics: relationships between school, home and neighbourhood; youth clubs and voluntary organisations; the health of children at school and young people at work; and 'compensatory' further education for workers in routine jobs. The main conclusion about education and employment was that purely educational aims came first: schools should not prepare pupils for particular types of employment; industry itself benefited from the teaching and learning of basic educational skills.

1948 CLARKE – OUT OF SCHOOL (CACE England)

Following up some of the conclusions of the first CACE report (see 1947 Clarke) this inquiry considered 'the natural interests and pursuits of school children out of school hours'. It urged that LEAs increase and improve facilities for children's play and recreation outside school hours, and that the government give financial support to voluntary bodies serving the out-of-school interests of school children. It further recommended that LEAs provide training courses for parents and all those who work with children.

1949 EVANS/AARON – THE FUTURE OF SECONDARY EDUCATION IN WALES (CACE Wales)

The report from this investigation made detailed recommendations for the organisation and curriculum of secondary education in Wales under the 1944 Education Act, and its relationship with primary and further education. It argued that education should be child-centred; it could take the form of either 'multilateral' schools or a dual system of grammar/technical schools and modern/technical schools (rather than a tripartite system), but must take into account variation in ability and aptitude between children. It recommended that the curriculum should emphasise free creation and cooperative inventiveness rather than passive assimilation, and that the study of history, geography and literature should give a central place to Wales. Particular attention was given to two issues: the rural and sparsely populated character of much of Wales, and the problems caused by the prevalence in Wales of two languages. As regards the latter, the committee recommended concentration on the pupil's first language, be it Welsh or English, with emphasis on conversation and oral work, but with a due subordinate place for written work. It argued that English must be taught well in predominantly Welsh-speaking areas, and the Welsh should be available as an option for all children in predominantly English-speaking areas.

1954 GURNEY-DIXON – EARLY LEAVING (CACE England)

This Committee considered the factors influencing the age at which pupils left 'secondary schools which provide courses beyond the minimum school leaving age' – in practice, grammar schools. Research was commissioned, with data being gathered principally from a 10% sample of all grammar schools, whose headmasters supplied details of the 'background, school record and potentialities' of the 1946 intake. The report concluded that a pupil's performance was closely related to his or her father's occupational status: the higher that status, the better a pupil's performance, not only in leaving school less early but in having a better academic record and, in the headmaster's judgement, more 'promise'. These differences increased during secondary education; children from lower-status occupational groups declined from their 11-plus position relative to higher groups. The report offered some speculative explanations of these differences, most involving aspects of home background, including shortage of money, 'bad living conditions', and lack of educational experience and unfavourable attitudes to education among parents in the lower-status occupational groups. This was the first major investigation of the working of the 1944 Education Act (see Chapter 4), and it cast doubt on the effectiveness of the Act in reducing social-class-based inequalities in education. It recommended that more grammar school places be provided, and that financial provision be improved for pupils who remained at school after the minimum leaving age.

1955 UNDERWOOD – MALADJUSTED CHILDREN

The term 'maladjusted children' entered common usage after the 1944 Education Act, and it was the aim of this committee to investigate the education of such children. Recommendations included the use of day, rather than boarding, schools wherever possible; the setting up of a comprehensive Child Guidance Service in every LEA, with a strengthened role for educational psychologists; and the introduction of preventive measures such as increased nursery provision.

1959 CROWTHER – 15 TO 18 (CACE England)

The Crowther committee was set up to consider the education of boys and girls between the ages of 15 and 18, and it was specifically asked to make recommendations about the place therein of exams below GCE level. The extensive research that was commissioned confirmed earlier findings (see 1954 Gurney-Dixon) about the relationship between father's occupational status and pupils' educational attainment. The higher the father's status, the greater the child's chance of attending a grammar rather than a secondary modern school, though the occupational group 'skilled manual workers' was so large that their children were by far the largest single group in all types of school. It was argued that there was considerable 'wastage' of talent, and much attention was paid to the 'neglected educational territory' of pupils who left school at 15 to follow a craft or technical, rather than an academic, career. The report recommended that there should be more further education. Of 16–18-year-olds, half should be in full-time further education by 1979, compared with 12% at the time of the report. [In the event, major expansion in further education came slightly later, in the 1980s, with high unemployment of school leavers and such schemes as YTS.] It accepted that some comprehensive schools could be set up, but on the whole endorsed the existing tripartite system, and indeed suggested further divisions within it (and within further education). The report argued that, in secondary modern schools, the top third of pupils were capable of taking and benefiting from external exams below GCE level [the future CSE, first examined in 1965], but that the majority of pupils there should be spared them. It was also recommended that early subject specialisation should be discouraged (although study in depth was still desirable in the sixth form); and that two sections from the 1994 Act which affected older pupils should be implemented, namely the raising of the school leaving age to 16 and compulsory part-time further education in county colleges. [The school leaving age was eventually raised, in 1972, but compulsory part-time further education has not been introduced.]

1960 ALBEMARLE – THE YOUTH SERVICE IN ENGLAND AND WALES

This committee was set up to review the Youth Service, which was thought to be demoralised and unprepared to deal with the increasing demand from the 'baby boom' children who were reaching adolescence. It recommended better training and status for youth leaders, a building programme of new premises and facilities, and the setting up of a Youth Service Development Council. It supported the continuation of a mixture of statutory and voluntary provision. [Most of the recommendations were implemented: the Development Council was set up to advise on a 10-year development programme; a large amount of building work was authorised and a special college opened in Leicester to train youth leaders, whose numbers doubled by 1966.]

1963 NEWSOM – HALF OUR FUTURE (CACE England)

This investigation considered the education of pupils between 13 and 16 of average and less than average ability. The terms of reference show some overlap with those of the Crowther Committee; there was considerable overlap in the pool of CACE research on which the two committees drew, and some similarity in the recommendations offered (see 1959 Crowther). Like Crowther, Newsom accepted the tripartite system, believing there to be different levels of natural ability in children which could best be catered for by different kinds of school. But it did not accept that schools for the less able should be poorer in buildings, quality of teaching, or any other respect. It recommended maintenance of existing structures, but with a redistribution of spending to the benefit of the less able (for example, the rebuilding of inadequate secondary modern schools in slum areas). Again like Crowther, it strongly recommended the raising of the school leaving age to 16 [this eventually happened in 1972] and the provision of a more stimulating and demanding curriculum so that pupils had a wider choice of courses, including some 'broadly related to occupational interests', and others concerned with personal and social development, and 'imaginative experience through the arts'. It advised that all 16-year-old school leavers should be provided with some form of 'internal leaving certificate' containing a 'general school record'. [In practice, the curriculum for many less able and average pupils became geared towards the new external CSE exam, contrary to Newsom's explicit recommendation. Only in the late 1970s did many schools begin to use pupil profiles and records of achievement similar to those Newsom had recommended.] Other miscellaneous recommendations were offered, including the provision of adequate religious instruction and positive guidance on sexual behaviour, the extension of the school day for older pupils, and the establishment of an experimental building programme 'to try out different forms of school organisation and teaching methods in buildings designed for the purpose'.

1963-4 ROBBINS - HIGHER EDUCATION
(Cmnd. 2154)

Appointed to review the pattern of full-time higher education in Great Britain, and advise on its long-term development, this committee commissioned extensive new research and examination of existing research. Looking particularly at entry into higher education, it found, like previous reports (see 1954 Gurney-Dixon, 1959 Crowther, 1963 Newsom), a high correlation between social class and educational achievement. (At the extremes, a child of professional parents was about 20 times more likely than a child of semi-skilled and unskilled workers to enter full-time higher education.) Even with controls for measured intelligence, the correlation remained high. The *proportions* of children from each class entering higher education remained much as in the 1920s, although the *absolute numbers* had increased steadily with the expansion of educational provision. However, social-class influence on attainment seemed to cease with university entry: once admitted, working-class students performed as well as middle-class students. Robbins concluded that there was a huge, untapped, and indeed often unsuspected 'pool of ability' in the population, especially in lower socioeconomic groups. It recommended a massive expansion in higher education (from 216,000 places in 1962-3 to 390,000 in 1972-3 and 560,000 by 1980). Also recommended were: the establishment of the Council for National Academic Awards (CNAA) to grant degrees to students in non-university establishments [this happened the following year]; the raising of the status of teacher training colleges to colleges of education offering BEd degrees, and their integration into universities [the former has happened, but the latter only in part]; the granting of university status to the 10 colleges of advanced technology [this was accepted], and in due course to other colleges [this did happen eventually, in the 1990s]; and the establishment of special institutions for scientific and technological education and research (SISTERS) [this has not been implemented].

1967 PLOWDEN – CHILDREN AND THEIR PRIMARY SCHOOLS (CACE England)

The Plowden Report examined primary education in England 'in all its aspects'. Based on extensive research, it concluded that parents' attitudes to education were of supreme importance in influencing children's educational success – more so than the parents' educational or occupational status, than material circumstances at home, and than schools themselves. It approved of 'progressive', child-centred teaching methods, a broader curriculum and increased parental involvement; it recommended that schools should become more involved in their communities – suggesting that there should be positive discrimination to help schools in deprived or 'educational priority areas' (EPAs). It also recommended expansion of nursery provision, the ending of corporal punishment in primary schools, and greater attention to the needs of slow learners, handicapped children and the children of immigrants. It argued that more teachers should be encouraged into primary schools (especially men, graduates and those who had specialised in maths and science), and a new group of staff called 'teachers' aides' should be recruited with a similar status to nursery assistants [never widely implemented]. It suggested that primary education could be reorganised into first and middle schools. [The Plowden Report had a profound effect on the way both professionals and parents viewed primary education, but few of its practical recommendations were immediately acted upon. Teachers in 'difficult' schools received an extra £75 annually (as against £120 recommended by Plowden). An expansion of nursery provision did not begin until 1973 (and was cut back not long afterwards). Money was found for school building projects, especially in EPAs, but 10 years later 20% of all primary pupils were still being educated in pre-1903 buildings, many with outside lavatories. A programme of action research was set up to establish and monitor EPAs. The concept of greater parental involvement was favourably received, and this involvement has increased in the years since Plowden. Corporal punishment was forbidden in *all* state schools from 1987.]

1967 GITTINS – PRIMARY EDUCATION IN WALES (CACE Wales)

Set up at the same time as Plowden, with the same terms of reference and some overlap of membership, this report shared Plowden's philosophy of education, and reached similar general conclusions. (See 1967 Plowden.) In addition, it considered some specifically Welsh issues, mainly the prevalence of two languages in school and community, but also the existence of large rural areas with sparse population, and a high respect widely felt for education and for teachers. It recommended a considerable increase in the advisory staff employed by LEAs, and in in-service training for teachers; improved coordination of primary education in Wales; and the fostering of both Welsh and English, especially Welsh as a second language in predominantly English-speaking areas.

1968 NEWSOM – PUBLIC SCHOOLS COMMISSION, FIRST REPORT

This commission was set up by a Labour government to advise on the future of boarding public schools in the light of comprehensivisation. Public schools were defined as those belonging to the Headmasters' Conference, Governing Bodies Association or Governing Bodies of Girls' Schools Association. It concluded that they could be abolished, integrated into the maintained system, or allowed to remain but without their traditional tax privileges – though the commission's terms of reference favoured integration. It recommended, as a step towards integration, that a number of public schools should accept some of their pupils (eventually at least half) from maintained schools, using criteria of comprehensive selection and social needs (rather than selection according to ability); these pupils would receive financial assistance. These arrangements should be voluntary if possible, but statutory if necessary. [The recommendations met considerable opposition and were never implemented.]

1968 SUMMERFIELD – PSYCHOLOGISTS IN THE EDUCATION SERVICE

This report recommended that the educational psychologist's brief should be extended beyond the traditional testing and assessing of children plus some remedial teaching to include 'an extended range of treatment'. (Treatment had previously been the responsibility of the psychiatrist within the Child Guidance Service.) It also recommended an increase in the numbers of educational psychologists, aiming at a proportion of one per 10,000 children.

1968 DAINTON – THE FLOW OF CANDIDATES IN SCIENCE AND TECHNOLOGY INTO HIGHER EDUCATION

The swing away from science in the sixth forms of secondary schools, which ran counter to the expansion of science and technology in the universities, was the subject of this investigation. The report called for changes in the sixth form, with less specialisation and some mathematics for all pupils. [The recommendations were not well received, and came up against a shortage of appropriately qualified teachers and the determination on the part of the grammar and public schools to defend the notion of sixth form study in depth.]

1969 HASLEGRAVE – TECHNICAL COURSES AND EXAMINATIONS

The committee reviewed the training of technicians and recommended the establishment of a Technician Education Council and a Business Education Council, to oversee courses and examinations. [These were set up, and later amalgamated to form what is now the Business and Technology Education Council (BTEC).]

1970 DONNISON – PUBLIC SCHOOLS COMMISSION, SECOND REPORT

The terms of reference for this commission were similar to Newsom's in 1968, but concerned with independent day schools and direct grant schools. The report recommended that they should either admit pupils without charging fees and without selecting by ability, or forgo state aid. [Direct grant schools were required to choose either comprehensivisation or withdrawal of state aid in 1975.]

1972 JAMES – TEACHER EDUCATION AND TRAINING

The James Report examined the arrangements for the education, training and probation of teachers in England and Wales, looking at course content, the role of different types of institution, and the relationship between intending teachers and other students. It proposed a radical recorganisation of teacher training to involve three stages (referred to as 'cycles'): general higher education, professional training and in-service training. The first cycle could take the form of a degree or a new qualification, a two-year Diploma in Higher Education. The second cycle would consist of a year's professional studies followed by a year as a 'licensed' teacher (replacing the existing probationary year), after which students would be awarded a BA(Ed). The third cycle, of in-service training, should amount to at least a term's worth every seven years for all teachers in post. [There was strong opposition to the 'licensed teacher' proposal from the teachers' unions, and little action was taken to try to implement this. The principle of integrating teacher training into higher education was accepted by the government, and throughout the 1970s colleges of education merged with other FE establishments, such as technical and art colleges, to form colleges and institutes of higher education.]

1973 RUSSELL – ADULT EDUCATION: A PLAN FOR DEVELOPMENT

After examining non-vocational adult education in England and Wales, this report suggested little change in the existing division of responsibility for adult education between LEAs, the university extra-mural departments and voluntary bodies such as the WEA. However, it did recommend the establishment of a national development council, regional advisory councils, and local organisations in every LEA, with a strengthening of the role of central government in both financial support and guidance to LEAs. It advised that employees should have a right to paid educational leave, and also that adult education courses should charge fees, but that these should be small. [No action on the report was taken until 1977, when the Advisory Council for Adult and Continuing Education was set up: a central body like the proposed national development council but lacking the strong government support called for by the report. The local organisations have not been established.]

1974 FINER – ONE-PARENT FAMILIES

This report examined the particular needs and problems of one-parent families (one in 10 of families with children by 1971), and many of its recommendations had educational implications: expansion of day care and nursery provision, encouragement of pregnant schoolgirls to continue their education, radical changes in the secondary school curriculum and in the careers guidance offered to girls to enable them to compete equally for better paid, traditionally male jobs, greater home–school contact with more support from guidance staff for children known to be in one-parent families. [The Finer Report was not debated in Parliament until over a year after it was published, and few of its recommendations on housing, law and benefits were implemented. The Sex Discrimination Act of 1975 provided the legal basis for equal opportunities for girls, but the 'radical changes' in girls' curriculum choices have not yet been introduced. Nursery and day care provision have expanded but still do not meet the demand. Care for school-age children outside school hours and in the holidays has received little attention. Little information is available on the extent to which schools are aware of, and providing for, the special needs of children from one-parent families, which now form a fifth of all families with children.]

1974 SWANN – THE FLOW INTO EMPLOYMENT OF SCIENTISTS, ENGINEERS AND TECHNOLOGISTS

A parallel report to Dainton (see 1968 Dainton), Swann investigated the flow of science and engineering graduates out of, rather than into, higher education. It concluded that the best graduates in these subjects tended to stay on at university rather than go into industry or teaching. It recommended that, in postgraduate training, there should be more emphasis on the links between the academic world and industry, and that scientists should be encouraged, in various ways, to contribute to the work of schools.

1975 BULLOCK – A LANGUAGE FOR LIFE

'All aspects of teaching the use of English, including reading, writing and speech' was the subject of this report. It was concerned mainly with England, though it took some evidence from other English-speaking countries (including Scotland). It emphasised that it was not concerned with reading alone, arguing that reading is not a discrete skill that can be considered in isolation from general language development. The evidence on standards of reading was examined: while the committee judged these inadequate for present-day society, they found no strong evidence of actual *decline*. The report provided a lengthy and thorough account of the acquisition and use of the entire range of language skills, stage by stage, from infancy to adulthood, and the problems and difficulties that can occur. Language teaching in 2,000 schools was surveyed: there was widespread commitment to basic skills, and much emphasis on formal practice. Insisting that there was no simple way in which reading and the use of English could be improved, and that improvement required 'a thorough understanding of the many complexities, and ... action on a broad front', the committee offered 333 conclusions and recommendations; only with reluctance was it prepared to select 17 of these as its principal findings. These included exhortations addressed to teachers, schools, LEAs and public attitudes, as well as direct recommendations to the government for specific action. The committee called for greater emphasis on language at all educational levels, with increased spending on staffing, accommodation and other resources. Detailed recommendations included: that every school should have a policy for 'language across the curriculum' and a suitably qualified teacher to support it, and that LEAs should appoint special advisers to support the schools; that there should be screening procedures to identify language difficulties at an early stage, and specialist assistance available at both school and LEA level for those in need; that language in education should form part of initial training for every teacher; that in-service education in reading and language should be expanded; and that a system of monitoring be set up, using new instruments to assess a wider range of attainments than in the past and establishing new criteria for literacy.

1975 ALEXANDER – ADULT EDUCATION: THE CHALLENGE OF CHANGE

After investigating voluntary, non-vocational adult education in Scotland, the committee recommended that adult education should be combined with the youth and community service into a community education service. [Most Scottish education authorities adopted this arrangement.]

1976 COWAN – REORGANISATION OF SECONDARY EDUCATION IN NORTHERN IRELAND

Ways of changing the Northern Ireland bipartite selective system (of grammar and secondary intermediate schools) to a non-selective system were investigated. The adoption of a dual system of 11–16 and 11–18 comprehensive schools was recommended; the former could have a two-form entry, but the latter required a six-form entry. Pupils could transfer from 11–16 to 11–18 schools for sixth-form courses. [These proposals were widely opposed, and they were abandoned by the new Conservative government in 1979, although much groundwork had been done in the meantime on the legal and administrative aspects of implementing them (see 1979 Benn, 1979 Dickson).]

1977 TAYLOR – A NEW PARTNERSHIP FOR OUR SCHOOLS

The arrangements for the 'management and government' of maintained schools in England and Wales were examined. It was recommended that every school have its own governing body, consisting of equal numbers of representatives of the LEA, school staff (including the headteacher *ex officio*), parents ('with, where appropriate, pupils') and the local community. The report suggested that all the powers relevant to school government should be formally vested in the LEA, but that it should delegate these as far as possible to the governing body of each school, who should in turn allow as much discretion as possible to the head. Specifically, governors should be given responsibility for defining the broad aims of the school; they in turn should invite the head and staff to devise means of pursuing them, and should themselves monitor the school's progress towards them. LEAs should provide initial and in-service training courses for governors, and all governors should attend them. [The main recommendations were implemented in the 1980 Education Act, and further extended in the 1986 Education Act; but the 1988 Education Reform Act introduced radical changes in the relationships between parents, governors, teachers, LEAs and central government (see Chapter 4).]

1977 MUNN – THE STRUCTURE OF THE CURRICULUM

Munn and Dunning are usually, and reasonably, considered together (see also 1977 Dunning). They were set up in close succession by the Secretary of State for Scotland to study the curriculum (Munn) and assessment (Dunning) in the third and fourth years of Scottish secondary schools; they kept in close touch with each other throughout their deliberations; and they presented their reports with complementary recommendations at the same time. The Munn Committee identified a number of problems with, and criticisms of the traditional Scottish secondary curriculum, notably those arising from two major recent developments, the rapid expansion of comprehensive schools, and the raising of the school leaving age to 16. These had left too many pupils of average ability or below either struggling with work beyond their abilities or following 'improvised' courses. For pupils of high ability, too much of the curriculum was often taken up with preparation for exams, and too little done to stretch them in the earlier years. At the same time, new subjects were being urged for inclusion in the school curriculum. The committee recommended that the curriculum in these two years should consist of a *core* and an *elective* area. The core would consist of seven subjects, four (English, maths, PE and RE) to be taken by all pupils, the other three (a social studies subject, a science, and a creative arts subject) to be chosen from a short list. The elective area would be wide-ranging, and a further two or three options would be chosen from it. Each course should have three syllabuses of different (but overlapping) levels of difficulty to cater for pupils of different ability, with some limited opportunities for transfer between them. The first year of secondary schooling, at 12 plus in Scotland, ought not to differentiate pupils, the committee thought, but differentiation should begin in the second year, and be well established by the third. [Unlike that of England and Wales, Scotland's 'national curriculum' has not been established by law, and how much influence Munn has actually had on schools is uncertain.] (See also Chapter 10, Figure 10.3.)

1977 DUNNING – ASSESSMENT FOR ALL

The Dunning Report on assessment should be taken together with the Munn Report on curriculum (see 1977 Munn). Dunning considered the assessment of third- and fourth-year pupils of all levels of academic ability in Scottish secondary schools. The committee recommended that O grades, taken only by the abler pupils, be replaced by an examination that matched comprehensive education, and that all pupils should be assessed for a single national certificate in each subject. To cater for pupils of different ability, however, and to ensure that everyone could gain a certificate, Dunning endorsed Munn's proposal for three syllabuses of different levels of difficulty, and recommended that certificates should be awarded at three corresponding levels, covering the entire ability range. These were termed Credit (the highest), General and Foundation, the last of these to be divided into Pass and CC (Course Completed). Awards should be based on continuous assessment of course work as well as on a final external examination. [The major recommendations of the Dunning Committee were accepted, and embodied in the Standard grade examination system, which has replaced O grades in Scotland (see Chapter 9).]

1978 OAKES – THE MANAGEMENT OF HIGHER EDUCATION IN THE MAINTAINED SECTOR

This report identified the principal tasks for management as gathering information on supply and demand, planning for change, allocating resources and general supervision. It proposed a new division of responsibility for finance between central and local government, and a structure of regional and national bodies to advise both the Secretary of State and LEAs on management tasks, while leaving considerable freedom of decision with both the LEAs and individual institutions.

1978 WADDELL – SCHOOL EXAMINATIONS

This report stemmed from the recommendation of the Schools Council in the early 1970s that the dual examination system of GCE and CSE should be replaced by a single system at 16 plus. The committee agreed that a single system was desirable, and suggested ways in which it could be implemented without excessive financial or administrative difficulty. They recommended using three modes, as in CSE, and a single grading system, though with special papers in some subjects for pupils of low or high ability. There should be regional groupings of GCE and CSE exam boards (four in England, one in Wales). They suggested that the unified courses could be offered from 1983, with the first exams in 1985. [In the event, the first GCSE courses were introduced in 1986, and the first exams took place in 1988. (See Chapter 9.)]

1978 WARNOCK – SPECIAL EDUCATIONAL NEEDS

The Warnock Report reviewed educational provision in Great Britain for children and young people 'handicapped by disabilities of body or mind'. It introduced the concept of 'special educational needs', recommending that it replace categorisation of children by the 10 existing statutory categories of handicap. It suggested that up to 20% of the school population might have such needs at some time in their school career (previously around 2% of children had been legally classed as 'handicapped'). It also recommended that children whose needs could not be met within the resources of the ordinary school should have a record (which came to be called a 'statement') of their special educational needs drawn up by a multiprofessional team. A detailed procedure was proposed for assessing and 'statementing' children with special educational needs, with parents having rights to be involved and make known their views. Wherever possible, children with special needs should be educated in ordinary schools alongside their peers (the principle of integration). [The Warnock Report strongly influenced the 1981 Education Act; see Chapter 4. See also Chapters 5 and 11 for further information about the education of children with special needs.]

1979 KEOHANE – PROPOSALS FOR A CERTIFICATE OF EXTENDED EDUCATION (Cmnd. 7755)

The purpose of this study was: to examine proposals (from the Schools Council) for a certificate of extended education (CEE) – a single-subject qualification at 17 plus, for pupils staying on after the compulsory leaving age but not taking A levels; to study pilot schemes already in operation; and to advise the Secretary of State as to whether the CEE should be given official recognition. The report recommended approval and development on a national basis, but with modifications so as to ensure that those taking the courses were prepared for employment. The committee felt that basic communication and numeracy skills were most important for this purpose, and so it was suggested that all CEE certificates should record proficiency scores in English and mathematics. In addition, it suggested that more courses should be developed that related directly to the world of work, and had titles informative to employers. The committee did not endorse the Schools Council's wish to see CEE courses closely linked to CSE courses and grades; it would prefer to see CEE courses more closely linked to FE courses (themselves in need of a simpler structure) and more vocational in emphasis.

1979 MANSELL - A BASIS FOR CHOICE

This was a report of a DES study group set up to consider full-time courses (mainly one-year courses) for young people of average ability and attainment, who had left school and needed neither GCE studies nor preparation for specific jobs. The group found that many such courses existed, but that they lacked coordination. It therefore recommended a unifying and rationalising curriculum structure, in the form of a set of criteria that existing and future courses might satisfy, with national validation but allowing scope for flexibility and local initiative. It was suggested that courses should consist of three main elements. First, there should be a common core of general education, occupying 50–60% of the course. The remainder should be tailored more to the vocational interests of the students, and be divided equally between vocational studies related to a general idea of employment and studies specific to a particular job. Students' final assessment should take the form of a profile, recording course work and subjective evaluations of abilities as well as the results of objective tests. A nationally recognised qualification should be awarded on successful completion of a validated course. The study group emphasised three principles underlying their recommendations: though not requiring an initial vocational commitment from students, courses must encourage the development of 'a realistic vocational focus' as they progress; attainment in vocational studies should receive equal recognition with academic attainment, and should not restrict future prospects; and the experience of learning is important in itself, as well as the attainment of certain levels of performance.

1979 ASTIN - REPORT OF THE WORKING PARTY ON THE MANAGEMENT OF SCHOOLS IN NORTHERN IRELAND

Set up after publication of the Taylor Report for England and Wales (see 1977 Taylor), this working party recommended that each school in Northern Ireland too (with the possible exception of small primary schools) should have a board of governors.

1979 BENN - REPORT OF THE WORKING PARTY ON VOLUNTARY SCHOOLS

This report investigated ways of allowing voluntary schools in Northern Ireland to continue (as direct grant schools) in the new non-selective system of secondary education recommended in the Cowan Report (see 1976 Cowan). [It became inapplicable when, after a change of government in 1979, the Cowan recommendations were abandoned.]

1979 DICKSON – REPORT ON PREPARATORY AND BOARDING DEPARTMENTS; REPORT ON THE STAFFING OF SECONDARY SCHOOLS; REPORT ON IN-SERVICE TRAINING

These were reports of investigations of various legal and administrative aspects of the new non-selective system of secondary education recommended in the Cowan Report (see 1976 Cowan). [They became inapplicable when, after a change of government in 1979, the Cowan recommendations were abandoned.]

1980 CHILVER – THE FUTURE STRUCTURE OF TEACHER EDUCATION IN NORTHERN IRELAND

An interim report of the Higher Education Review Group for Northern Ireland (see also 1982 Chilver), Chilver investigated implications for the teacher education system of falling school rolls. It recommended that the three Belfast teacher training colleges come together on a single site. [The proposal aroused strong opposition from both Catholic and Protestant churches, and was not adopted.]

1981 RAMPTON – WEST INDIAN CHILDREN IN OUR SCHOOLS (Cmnd. 8273)

The 'Rampton Committee' was set up in 1979, late in the life of the Labour government (its membership was finalised by the new Conservative government), to investigate the education of children from all ethnic minority groups. First, though, it was required to produce an interim report on West Indian children. Research commissioned by the committee appeared to show considerable underachievement by West Indian children, on average, compared with White and Asian children. Various possible explanations were considered, with particular attention paid to racism, a factor frequently mentioned in evidence to the committee. While believing that few teachers were intentionally racist, and while not accepting that racism was the sole cause of West Indian underachievement, the committee concluded that unintentional racism (in the sense of stereotyped, negative or patronising views of West Indian children) was widespread and did influence children's performance. Other contributory causes that were suggested included the inadequacy of preschool provision and its particular unsuitability for West Indian families; prejudice on the part of some teachers against West Indian children's use of English;

inappropriate curricula and teaching materials; and the discouraging effect of the relatively poor employment prospects of West Indian school leavers resulting from discrimination in the labour market. At the same time, the committee believed, some West Indian parents did not do enough to support schools and teachers. In a long list of detailed recommendations, the committee urged institutions and organisations at all levels to recognise these problems and work to solve them. The main requirement, as they saw it, was for a change in attitude in the community at large towards acceptance of ethnic minorities. In specifically educational matters, stress was laid on both initial and in-service training of teachers to attune them to the needs of ethnic minority groups and to improve their understanding of a multicultural approach to education. (For the final report of this committee, see 1985 Swann.)

1982 CHILVER – THE FUTURE OF HIGHER EDUCATION IN NORTHERN IRELAND

This was the final report of the Higher Education Educational Review Group for Northern Ireland (see also 1980 Chilver). It set out to predict likely demand for higher education until the end of the century, and to provide guidelines for meeting it. Recommendations were that the New University of Ulster move towards more emphasis on mature students, distance learning and non-degree work; that Ulster Polytechnic increase emphasis on vocational studies; and that Queen's University Belfast continue largely as before, though with more emphasis on broadly based and part-time courses, and, where possible, three-year degree courses (instead of four-year). [In the event, the New University of Ulster and Ulster Polytechnic amalgamated in 1985 to form the University of Ulster.]

1982 COCKROFT – MATHEMATICS COUNTS

The subject of this investigation was mathematics teaching in primary and secondary schools in England and Wales, in the light of the mathematical needs of pupils when they proceed to further or higher education, employment and adult life generally. It attempted to identify these needs, and addressed detailed recommendations for meeting them to central government, LEAs, examination boards, teachers, training institutions and funding bodies for research and curriculum development. More general recommendations were addressed to the public at large. These included: that the diversity of pupils' abilities should be recognised, and a 'differentiated curriculum' and range of examination papers provided; that the quality of the maths teaching force be improved – by the recruitment and retention of more well-qualified mathematicians through financial incentives, flexible salary structures and guarantees of employment, and through increases in in-service training and support; that the subject should be approached by teachers in a variety of different ways, including exposition, discussion, practical work and problem-solving, as well as mental and oral work; and that curriculum materials be developed reflecting a 'foundation list' of mathematical topics identified by the committee.

1982 SWINNERTON-DYER – THE SUPPORT OF UNIVERSITY SCIENTIFIC RESEARCH

This report investigated postgraduate education, especially as supported by such bodies as the Science and Engineering Research Council and the Social Science Research Council, and its success in meeting national manpower requirements. It recommended that the councils monitor the rates of submission of theses by research students in every university, so as to be able to impose sanctions on universities whose rates were unsatisfactory. It was also recommended that the DES should encourage postgraduate conversion courses, by means of maintenance grants, and that a single national body should be set up to identify manpower requirements and commission courses to meet them.

1982 THOMPSON – EXPERIENCE AND PARTICIPATION

This was a review of the Youth Service, set up by the recently elected Conservative government. It recommended that a government minister be appointed to coordinate the work of all departments concerned with youth affairs, and that there should be more funding and clearer national objectives. It suggested that the Youth Service should be attempting to meet the 'crucial social needs' of the 11–20 age group, especially the unemployed, the handicapped, girls and young women, and ethnic minorities. [Most of the report's recommendations were rejected in the government's formal response two years later.]

1985 SWANN – EDUCATION FOR ALL
(Cmnd. 9453)

Just before what had been the Rampton Committee published its interim report (see 1981 Rampton), Mr Antony Rampton was replaced as chairman by Lord Swann. The final report – almost eight times as long as the interim – was able to cover the same ground in more detail and also to extend the coverage to a wide range of ethnic minority groups. Further research studies confirmed the earlier picture of West Indian pupils' underachievement, on average, compared with Asian and White pupils, but showed that the gap appeared to be diminishing significantly as time passed. The committee remained convinced that largely unintentional racism was an important factor behind West Indian underachievement, a claim not undermined by the high achievement of Asians, since stereotyped views of them were generally much less negative, and racism might have different effects on different groups. Of other possible causes of these disparities in achievement, IQ differences were considered at length, but not found to be a significant factor. Differences in socioeconomic conditions, however, were found to provide a partial explanation for the relatively low attainment not only of West Indian but probably also of Bangladeshi children. Socioeconomic differences themselves often resulted from racial discrimination, especially in employment and housing. The committee also considered, rather more briefly, the educational needs of Chinese, Cypriot, Italian, Ukrainian and Vietnamese children, and the particular needs of Travellers' children and 'Liverpool Blacks'. The committee's general conclusion was that the response to these issues must lie in the education of all children, not just of ethnic minority children. All LEAs and schools must lead pupils to understand what is involved in Britain's being a multiracial and multicultural society; this must permeate all the work of schools. Racism must be fought, and inherited myths and stereotypes attacked. More detailed recommendations included giving first priority in language teaching to English. Although linguistic diversity was considered a positive asset, bilingualism in maintained schools was not supported. Separate schools for ethnic groups, though permissible in law, were not supported either. The committee believed that if its proposals were adopted, the demand for such schools would be greatly reduced. In this connection, central government and LEAs were urged to be sensitive to the wishes of some groups to have their daughters educated in single-sex schools. It suggested that more attention should be given to multicultural matters in both initial training and in-service training of teachers, and that the effectiveness of racism awareness training should be investigated. It further recommended that greater effort should be made to employ and promote teachers from ethnic minority groups, though without positive discrimination or lowering of standards.

1985 LINDOP – ACADEMIC VALIDATION IN PUBLIC SECTOR HIGHER EDUCATION

This report recommended a variety of methods of validation. It suggested that some polytechnics and colleges should be given complete autonomy by the Secretary of State to validate their own courses; others should be allowed more limited autonomy, in specific areas; while in yet others external validation should remain. It also proposed that there should be a national organisation to coordinate the activities of universities in validating public sector colleges' degree courses. [Since 1992, all polytechnics – now universities – and several colleges have autonomy to validate their courses.]

1987 BLACK – NATIONAL CURRICULUM TASK GROUP ON ASSESSMENT AND TESTING: A REPORT

As part of the preparations for what became the 1988 Education Reform Act (see Chapter 4), the Government set up a Task Group on Assessment and Testing (TGAT), under the chairmanship of Professor Paul Black, to devise assessment arrangements, stipulating that pupils should be assessed at the end of each of four *key stages*, at the ages of seven, 11, 14 and 16 respectively. The TGAT recommended that at the first key stage, assessment should only be in the core subjects of the national curriculum (English, mathematics and science plus Welsh in Welsh-speaking schools in Wales). At subsequent key stages it should be in all the foundation subjects (the core subjects plus art, geography, history, music, physical education, technology, a modern foreign language at the last two stages, and Welsh in non-Welsh speaking schools in Wales). At the first three key stages, assessment should be formative for individual pupils; at the final stage it should also be summative. At each stage, the pupils should be assessed against appropriate *attainment targets*, grouped into a small number (the Task Group recommended no more than four) of *profile components*, reflecting the range of knowledge, skills and understanding the subject encompasses. For each profile component, there should be a progression through criterion-referenced *levels* of achievement – 10 levels for subjects taught throughout the full age range of five to 16. The same scale of levels should be used to assess children at every stage. This would allow direct comparison of the attainments of all children, regardless of age, and, it was argued, make children themselves more aware of their progress over the years. Assessment should combine two different methods: first, the teachers' judgments of their pupils' attainments, based on their work in class; and secondly, the pupils' performance on *standard assessment tasks* (SAT) set nationally. A wide range of SATs should be available, from which teachers could select so as to be able to incorporate them into the work they and their pupils were doing, and use them for formative and diagnostic as well as summative purposes. Procedures should be established for monitoring teachers' assessments, especially where they disagreed with the SAT results. At the final key stage (age 16), assessment should, for the present, be through the existing GCSE examinations (see Chapter 9), though this would eventually need to be modified. The results for individual children should be kept confidential, and made available only to their parents and teachers. But aggregated test results – by class and by school – should be published for Key Stages 2, 3 and 4, to enable parents to judge how well teachers and schools were performing. However, such results should be published only as part of a broader report – by a school about its work as a whole, and by the local authority about the socioeconomic characteristics of the area that are known to affect schools' and children's performance. [Most of the recommendations of the TGAT Report were initially accepted by the Secretary of State – though aggregated results for schools were published in the form of 'league tables', and not only in the context of reports by schools and LEAs. The TGAT model was used as a framework by the national curriculum subject working groups in drawing up programmes of study and attainment targets. But the assessment arrangements were widely criticised as too complicated, time-consuming and costly – criticisms ministers came to share. In addition, ministers became uneasy about the TGAT's concern with formative and diagnostic as against summative testing, and its emphasis on the judgements of teachers. Over the next few years, teachers' assessments were reduced in importance, as compared with external national tests. The wide range of SATs originally proposed was replaced by a narrower range of more limited tests, simpler and quicker to administer. Some changes were made to the TGAT framework: for example, attainment targets were no longer grouped into profile components, but were themselves divided into *strands*. Finally, still more simplification of the system of national assessment was proposed in the Dearing Report and accepted by the Secretary of State. See 1994 Dearing, and Chapter 10 below.]

1988 KINGMAN – REPORT OF THE COMMITTEE OF INQUIRY INTO THE TEACHING OF ENGLISH LANGUAGE

The committee was established to recommend a model of how the English language (whether spoken or written) works, which would form a basis for teacher training and professional discussion of English teaching; to recommend how and how far this model should be made explicit to pupils; and to recommend what pupils should be taught and be expected to understand by the ages of seven, 11 and 16. The model recommended is in four parts. The first describes the *forms* of English, spoken and written, at various levels from individual letters or sounds to connected discourse. These include vowel and consonant sounds, intonation and stress; the alphabet, spelling and punctuation; the formation of plurals and comparatives, and the use of metaphors and idiomatic expressions; the structure of phrases and sentences, the characteristics of verbs (such as tense, aspect, mood and number agreement), nouns, adjectives, adverbs, adjuncts, disjuncts and conjuncts; and the structure of units of discourse larger than the sentence. The second part describes *communication* by speakers or writers and *comprehension* by listeners or readers. This includes consideration of the context and type of discourse, of the intentions and attitudes of both speaker and listener, and of various processes of inference used in deriving meaning from sounds, forms and contexts. The third part describes the ways in which children *acquire* the forms of language, and *develop* their ability to use and understand them, with consideration of what might be found easy or difficult at different stages of development. The fourth part describes *variation* in English, over time and from place to place. Other dialects and creole languages differ systematically from Standard English; their forms and phrases are not 'bad grammar'. The report recommends that children should learn to write clearly and accurately in Standard English, and argues that they can be helped in this by learning to use descriptive technical terms to talk about language. But it does not favour a return to 'old-fashioned formal teaching of grammar' or learning by rote. How explicit the report's own model of language should be made to *pupils*, and when, is a matter for the professional judgement of teachers. The report favours the setting of attainment targets for children at seven, 11 and 16 (though with some publicly expressed reservations by Sir John Kingman himself about whether English can be 'mastered rung by rung' as in climbing a ladder (Nash, 1988)), and spells out in some detail what these should be. At all three stages, these targets include both skills in *using* English, and explicit knowledge *about* the language – its rules and conventions, its historical and geographical variation, and so on. Considerable attention is paid to the linguistic knowledge and skills required of teachers, and the ways in which these can best be learnt. Detailed recommendations are made about the amount and kind of training in English language teaching appropriate for primary teachers, and for English teachers and teachers of other subjects in secondary schools; the report's own model is recommended as a basis for these. As well as occupying a more important place in initial teacher training, English language should become one of the 'national priority areas' for in-service training of teachers.

1988 HIGGINSON – ADVANCING A LEVELS

The committee was set up to examine the principles that should govern GCE A-level syllabuses and their assessment. It recommended a thorough revision of present arrangements. There should be more coordination of the work of the GCE examining boards, with more uniform standards of marking, a reduction in the number of separate syllabuses in each subject and a compulsory core common to the remaining syllabuses. A fifth of A-level assessment should be based on course work rather than the final examination. The recommendation most widely noticed was that full-time students should normally study a wider range of subjects – five A levels plus one AS level, rather than three A levels as at present. [The recommendations of the report were rejected by the Secretary of State immediately on its publication.]

1989 ELTON – DISCIPLINE IN SCHOOLS

The committee was established to recommend action to secure the orderly atmosphere necessary in schools for teaching and learning. It judged the main discipline problem facing teachers to be not the rare serious incidents of physical aggression, but the cumulative disruptive effects of relatively trivial but persistent misbehaviour. It offered no simple diagnosis of causes, or simple remedies, but instead made a wide range of recommendations to teachers, headteachers, governing bodies, LEAs and parents. Central to these were ways of helping teachers become more effective classroom managers – in both initial and in-service training. Others include the following. Schools should attempt to create a positive atmosphere based on a sense of community and shared values. Heads' management styles should encourage a sense of collective responsibility among teachers, and of commitment to school among pupils and parents; their management training should be directed towards this. School buildings should be kept in a good state of repair and appearance. Parents need to provide their children with firm guidance and positive models of behaviour; schools should do more to prepare pupils for the responsibilities of being parents. Pupils themselves should be given more responsibility, and their non-academic achievements should be given more recognition.

1992 HOWIE – UPPER SECONDARY EDUCATION IN SCOTLAND

The Howie Committee was set up in 1990 to review the curriculum and examinations in the fifth and sixth years of secondary education in Scotland. The Committee was highly critical of present arrangements. It concluded that the curricular breadth on which Scotland prides itself is not reflected in actual attainment. Many pupils obtain only one or two Highers, and many others none at all. Even the ablest pupils compare badly in breadth of attainment with those in European countries. At the same time, Higher courses give little opportunity for study in depth, as pupils have to learn too much, too quickly after Standard grade (see Chapter 9 below), whose own pace is too slow. Many pupils are therefore insufficiently prepared for higher education. Vocational education is too sharply divided from academic education, and held in low esteem. There is too much flexibility, leading to arbitrary course choices and making coherent course planning difficult. To meet these criticisms, the Committee suggested that Standard grade courses should be started earlier and completed by the end of the third year; and that in the fourth, fifth and sixth years, pupils should follow one of two routes: either a one- or two-year programme leading to a Scottish Certificate (SCOTCERT); or a three-year programme leading to a Scottish Baccalaureate (SCOTBAC). The SCOTCERT programme would be aimed at the majority (60–70%) of fourth-year pupils, but would also be available to adults and in further education colleges. It would cover a combination of 'core skills', general education and vocational education, in a modular structure (with 16 modules per year). The modules would be based, in part, on existing National Certificate modules, and amalgamated with the new GSVQs (see Chapter 9 below). It would prepare pupils for employment, further training or more advanced education. The SCOTBAC programme would offer two 'lines of study', one in arts, the other in science, but with some academic and vocational variants. There would be a 'core' common to both lines (English, modern languages, mathematics, science, social subjects, music, art, history and information technology), but the weighting of subjects within the core would vary between the lines. In addition, there would be optional subjects, but these would be restricted in number and required to form a coherent programme of study (which could be vocational as well as academic in emphasis). Courses would be based, in part, on existing Higher and CSYS courses, but major core subjects would be taken to a level well beyond Higher and in some cases beyond CSYS level; optional subjects would be taken to at least Higher level. SCOTBAC would be the normal route to higher education. Assessment in both SCOTCERT and SCOTBAC would be criterion-referenced, and partly internal, partly external. The SCOTBAC would be awarded with an overall grade, on a scale A–D; pupils need not pass every subject, and good performance in some could to some extent outweigh poor performance in others. Arrangements should be made for pupils to be able to transfer between the two programmes. [Just over two years after the publication of the Report, the government published its response. By and large, it rejected the Howie recommendations, though they have had some influence on the government's own plans. Standard grade courses are to remain in the third and fourth years. For the fifth and sixth years, Highers will remain, but with modifications (see Chapter 9 below). The proposed 'twin-track' structure of SCOTCERT and SCOTBAC had met much opposition, on the grounds that SCOTBAC would inevitably be held in much higher esteem than SCOTCERT. As few schools would be able to offer both tracks, a system of 'SCOTBAC schools' and 'SCOTCERT schools' might develop. There would be strong parental pressure for pupils to attend the former, leading to high rates of drop-out or failure.]

1993 DEARING – THE NATIONAL CURRICULUM AND ITS ASSESSMENT

This is the final report, after consultations and an interim report, by an individual (Sir Ron Dearing, the Chairman of the School Curriculum and Assessment Authority), not a committee. Dearing was asked by the Secretary of State for Education to review the national curriculum with a view to 'slimming down' the curriculum, simplifying its assessment arrangements, considering the future of the 10-level scale of attainment, and improving the central administration. Dearing recommended that for these purposes there should be an immediate, closely coordinated review of the curriculum orders in all the subjects of the national curriculum. For Key Stages 1–3 (i.e. pupils aged five–14), these reviews should aim to reduce the statutory curriculum enough to free about 20% of teaching time for use at the discretion of schools. This reduction should be achieved, not by removing any subjects from the compulsory curriculum, or by altering the basic content of programmes of study, but by identifying an essential core for each subject, and reducing the number of attainment targets so as to concentrate on that core. Statements of attainment should also be reduced in number and made less specific, or perhaps even replaced by a smaller number of more general 'level descriptors'. Schools should use the discretionary time thus made available primarily for basic literacy, oracy and numeracy, and then for deepening pupils' knowledge and understanding of the national curriculum subjects. They should be accountable to their governing bodies for their use of this time. For Key Stage 4 (i.e. pupils aged 14–16), the schools' discretion should be extended. Only English, mathematics, science, and PE should be compulsory, together with short courses in a modern foreign language and (from 1996) technology; the remaining national curriculum subjects (art, geography, history and music) should be optional. (Dearing notes that religious education and sex education will also be compulsory at this stage, but outside the national curriculum.) For the teaching time thus freed, vocational as well as academic options should be considered. The 10-level scale of attainment should be retained for the subjects that use it, but it should be used only until the end of Key Stage 3. (The subjects that do not use the scale – art, music and PE – should continue to use end-of-key-stage statements instead.) The national curriculum thus revised should not be altered for five years. National tests should be simplified as far as possible without sacrificing validity or reliability; calls on teachers' time for administering tests, conducting teacher assessment and keeping records should be reduced. (Except for the core subjects in primary schools, statutory teacher assessment should be postponed until the curriculum had been slimmed down in accordance with the recommendations above.) The national curriculum and its assessment arrangements should continue to be available for pupils with special educational needs, and the levels defined in curriculum orders should be broadened to take account of this. Teachers of pupils with special needs should be consulted over this, and parents of pupils with special needs should be involved by schools in the development of appropriate curricula for their children. [These recommendations were accepted by the Secretary of State, with minor modifications and additions, the proposed reviews were duly conducted, and new draft curriculum orders were issued in May 1994, for consultation and planned implementation from August 1995 (see Chapter 10 below).]

1996 DEARING – REVIEW OF QUALIFICATIONS FOR 16–19-YEAR-OLDS

Dearing's recommendations included the following. The division between education and training should be replaced by a single national framework of qualifications for three types of course: *academic* and *applied* courses in schools and colleges, and *vocational* courses in places of work. As a consequence, the School Curriculum and Assessment Authority (SCAA) and the National Council for Vocational Qualifications (NCVQ) should be merged. The assessment of GNVQs should be simpler but more rigorous. They should be renamed 'Applied A levels' to indicate their comparability in standards with academic A levels. A levels (in single subjects) should be retained, but a National Advanced Diploma should be created, to recognise high achievement across a range of areas of study. AS levels should be based on the first half of A level syllabuses, thus enabling students who take them to keep open the options of proceeding to A level or to National Advanced Diploma courses. (Their name should be changed from 'Advanced Supplementary' to 'Advanced Subsidiary'.) Students should also be able to take a half-length and a quarter-length Advanced GNVQ (equivalent in standard to 1 A level and 1 AS level respectively). Young high achievers should be able to take university courses while remaining school pupils. Applied and vocational courses should be open to pupils as young as 14 who do not find school of relevance to them, while remaining school pupils. Pupils with learning difficulties should have courses to teach (and accredit) the skills necessary for leading independent adult lives. [Both the Conservative Government in office when Dearing reported and its Labour successor broadly accepted Dearing's recommendations. Some have already been implemented, notably the merger of SCAA and NCVQ as the Qualifications and Curriculum Authority (QCA). Several others were to have been implemented in 1998, but this was postponed by the new Government to allow a period of consultation about the main proposals: see Chapter 9 below.]

1997 DEARING – HIGHER EDUCATION IN THE LEARNING SOCIETY

This Dearing Report applies to higher education (HE) in the whole of the United Kingdom, though there is a supplementary report for Scotland by an offshoot of the Dearing Committee (see below 1997 Garrick). The main Report makes over ninety recommendations, addressed to the Government, HE institutions and others. These include the following:

• **Funding and participation** The Report notes that over the last 20 years, the number of students has more than doubled, while public funding of HE has increased by 45% in real terms, so that funding per student has fallen by 40%. HE institutions have coped, in part, by under-investment in infrastructure. The Government has responded to the increased demand, especially between 1988 and 1993, by capping any further growth in numbers of publicly funded, full-time undergraduate students, and withdrawing almost all public funding of capital expenditure. The Committee was concerned that short-term funding problems, and responses to them by Government and institutions, should not prejudice the long-term future of HE. It recommended that capping of student numbers should end, and HE resume its growth, but that students' contributions towards the cost of their own HE should be increased. Having considered several alternatives, the Committee recommended that the current system of support for students' living costs (50% grant and availability of 50% loan) be retained, but that a flat rate charge of 25% of tuition costs be introduced, to be paid by all graduates in work through an income-dependent mechanism run by the Inland Revenue. For the funding of institutions, there should be a shift away from block grants and towards 'following the student': by 2003, 60% of HE public funding should depend on students' choices.

- **Curriculum** Students should have a wider range of choice of types of course, including more courses offering breadth across different subjects rather than one subject in more depth. Institutions and employers should develop further the work experience component of HE courses. Institutions should specify the knowledge, understanding and skills (both general and subject specific) that students can be expected to have at the end of courses.
- **Qualifications** The Report proposes a new framework for HE qualifications throughout the UK, offering consistency, progression, breadth and intelligibility, encompassing both academic and educational qualifications, and allowing accredited stopping-off points, credit accumulation and credit transfer between institutions. It would consist of eight levels, following on from A level or the equivalent (see Chapter 9 below), with detailed specification of how these levels could be attained by single subjects or combinations of subjects, academic or professional studies, by taught courses or by research. Levels should normally be distinguished by achievement, and not by length of study required.

H1	Certificate
H2	Diploma
H3	Bachelor's degree
H4	Honours degree
H5	Higher Honours/Postgraduate Conversion Diploma
H6	Masters degree
H7	MPhil
H8	Doctorate

The operation of this framework should be monitored by the Quality Assurance Agency.

● **Teaching** Teaching in HE should be valued more highly as a profession in its own right, with its own professional body, the Institute of Learning and Teaching in Higher Education. The training of academic staff as teachers should be more focused, and in the medium term all new academic staff should be required to achieve membership of the Institute.

● **Northern Ireland** The Report notes that Northern Ireland (like Scotland) has a high participation rate in HE – 45% of young people, compared with 32% in the UK as a whole – but that not sufficient places are available for them all to study in Northern Ireland itself. (Currently only 60% of HE students do so.) Several options are suggested for increasing the number of places. Also, in reaffirming the value of the Government's use in Great Britain of intermediary funding bodies so as to remain 'at arm's length' from individual institutions, the Report recommends that the practice be extended to Northern Ireland.

[The Government responded favourably to the Report, accepting most of its recommendations at least in part or in principle. As regards student support, it accepted the Dearing proposal that students pay about a quarter of their tuition fees (assessed at a flat rate of £1000 per annum); this is to be paid 'upfront' on a means-tested basis. But contrary to Dearing's recommendation, it will not maintain the arrangement of 50% grant and 50% loan towards students' living costs, but move towards a system of loans only (with a transitional period and protection of the interests of current students). The available loans are to be increased, and students need not begin repaying them until they are earning an income of a specific level (currently at £10,000). As regards the framework for qualifications, the Government accepts this recommendation in principle, though not necessarily in detail. The details are to be left to HE institutions to decide, for implementation in 2000.]

1997 GARRICK – HIGHER EDUCATION IN THE LEARNING SOCIETY: REPORT OF THE SCOTTISH COMMITTEE

The Garrick Report is a supplement to the main Dearing Report (see above: 1997 Dearing), accepting most of the main Report's recommendations for the United Kingdom as a whole, and concentrating on Scottish issues. The Report notes the distinctiveness of Scottish HE in a number of respects. (1) Like Northern Ireland, Scotland has a high participation rate in HE – 45% of young people, compared with 32% in the UK as a whole. But in Scotland, a higher percentage of HE students are pursuing sub-degree qualifications – 40%, compared with 26% in the UK as a whole. (2) HE in Scotland is based on a broader school curriculum than in the rest of the UK: Scottish HE candidates typically study up to five or six subjects to Higher level, compared with a maximum of three subjects at A level elswhere. (3) Admission to Scottish universities is traditionally to a faculty rather than to a department, as elsewhere in the UK, allowing students greater flexibility and opportunity to change track. (4) The arts first degree at the older universities is called MA, not BA, with a three-year 'ordinary' and a four-year 'honours' version. The ordinary degree is still a valued qualification, and the degree of choice for many students. It is not regarded as a failed honours degree (as a 'pass' degree sometimes is elsewhere in the UK). However, the ordinary degree may be less valued by employers now than formerly. (5) There is a clearer division than in England between the traditional universities and the post-1993 universities (see Chapter 5), the latter being more distinctively vocational in character than in England. The Committee was anxious to maintain the distinctiveness of Scottish HE, and offered recommendations in parallel but not identical to those of Dearing for the rest of the UK. Distinctive proposals included the following. There should be a new, more consistent and intelligible, framework of qualifications for Scotland, similar to that recommended by Dearing but continuing to include the three-year ordinary degree (renamed BA) as 'an honourable exit point'. The student-elected rector in the four ancient universities (see Chapter 7) should no longer have the automatic right to chair the university court (the supreme decision-making body). Scottish students' total tuition fees for a four-year honours degree should not be greater than those elsewhere in the UK, where an honours degree course takes three years.

1997 KENNEDY – LEARNING WORKS

This was the final report (following an interim report *Pathways to Success*) of a committee appointed by the Further Education Funding Council (FEFC) to investigate under-participation in further education (FE) and make recommendations as to how participation might be increased. The committee's recommendations included the following. The government should develop a national strategy for post-16 learning, and publicly-funded FE should play a major part in this; market forces alone are insufficient. There should also be strategic partnerships at local level, with FE colleges given responsibilities for meeting the needs of their local communities. The different ways currently in existence for funding FE should be harmonised. Employers should be given financial incentives to help their employees with FE. The FEFC itself should alter its funding criteria to favour young people with lower levels of previous attainment and adults from economically deprived areas. Those who can afford to pay more towards the costs of their FE should do so, but tax relief should be available for this. A national system of information and guidance about FE should be established.

SOURCES AND FURTHER READING

Although official reports are usually best known by the names of the chairpersons of the committees of inquiry that produced them, they are rarely to be found under those names in the author indexes of libraries. The official authorship of reports is varied and sometimes confusing; usually the easiest way of finding official reports in libraries is to look under the titles in title indexes.

In addition to the reports themselves, the following are useful sources. Evans et al. (1994), contains summaries, mostly briefer than ours, of a wide, though still selective, range of reports, including a number not covered here. Corbett (1978) and Rogers (1980) have longer summaries and discussions than ours, but of a smaller number of reports, and of course do not cover the most recent reports.

Corbett, A. (1978) *Much To Do About Education*, 4th edn, London: Macmillan.

Evans, M. et al. (eds) (1994) *Education Yearbook 1995*, Harlow: Longman.

Gathorne-Hardy, J. (1977) *The Public School Phenomenon*, London: Hodder & Stoughton.

Gordon, P. and Lawton, D. (1984) *A Guide to English Educational Terms*, London: Batsford.

Mackinnon, D. (1976) *Social Class and Educational Attainment*, Milton Keynes: Open University Press (a component of OU Course E201 *Personality and Learning*).

Nash, I. (1988) Kingman sets stage for new English working party, *Times Educational Supplement*, 6 May 1988.

NICER (1984) *Register of Research 1978–82*, Belfast: Northern Ireland Council for Educational Research.

Rogers, R. (1980) *Crowther to Warnock: How Fourteen Reports Tried to Change Children's Lives*, London: Heinemann.

This chapter summarises the main Acts of Parliament concerned with or directly relevant to education, together with a small number of particularly important ministerial circulars, regulations and orders. It is inevitably highly selective, both in the Acts it covers and in what it includes from each Act. No attempt is made to use legally precise terms or statements in the summaries. We begin with the 1870 Education Act – which in many ways marks the beginning of the modern education system – but concentrate on legislation since 1944.

Except where otherwise specified, these Acts apply to England and Wales.

1870 ELEMENTARY EDUCATION ACT
('The Forster Act')

The aim of this Act was to provide elementary schools throughout the country, filling the gaps in the existing provision established by the churches, private benefactors and guilds. It divided the country into school districts, and, in those districts with inadequate provision, required school boards to be elected which would raise money through the rates to provide public elementary schools (often called 'board schools'). These schools were to be non-denominational and open to inspection. School boards were allowed to prescribe weekly fees and to pass byelaws requiring attendance by all children between five and 13 years of age.

1880 EDUCATION ACT (The 'Mundella Act')

This Act required school boards to pass byelaws to secure attendance (although pupils older than 10 could be exempted if they had achieved a certain standard of attainment, or a satisfactory record of attendance). Fees in elementary schools were limited to 9d per week.

1888 LOCAL GOVERNMENT ACT

This Act created county councils and county borough councils, which were later used as the framework for educational administration (see 1902 Education Act).

1891 EDUCATION ACT

In effect, this Act made elementary education free.

1892 EDUCATION ACT (IRELAND)

This introduced compulsory school attendance in Ireland, and required local authorities to create School Attendance Committees to enforce it.

1899 BOARD OF EDUCATION ACT

This Act set up a Board of Education to supervise the education system.

1902 EDUCATION ACT ('The Balfour Act')

The 1902 Act established a system of secondary education as the 1870 Act had done for elementary education, by filling the gaps in the existing provision with non-denominational state schools. The Act abolished the school boards and replaced them with a system of local education authorities based on the county and county borough councils of the 1880 Local Government Act. In the county areas, however, responsibility for elementary education was given to non-county boroughs with a population exceeding 10,000 and urban districts with a population in excess of 20,000. These were known as Part III Authorities (and were abolished by the 1944 Act).

The new LEAs took over the responsibility to provide adequate facilities for elementary education and in addition were authorised to provide 'education other than elementary', either by setting up new secondary schools or by aiding existing ones in their areas. They were allowed to raise and spend rates, within set limits, to fulfil these responsibilities. In some areas this resulted in generous secondary provision, whilst other areas did as little as possible. Section 6 of the Act stipulated that all elementary schools had to have managers and laid down how many of these should be LEA representatives. Governors for secondary schools were dealt with under regulations made under the Act between 1902 and 1908.

1906 EDUCATION (PROVISION OF MEALS) ACT

LEAs were authorised by this Act to spend public money on meals for under-nourished elementary school children.

1907 EDUCATION (ADMINISTRATIVE PROVISIONS) ACT

With this Act LEAs were required, for the first time, to provide for the medical inspection of children in elementary schools.

1910   EDUCATION (CHOICE OF EMPLOYMENT) ACT

By enabling LEAs, if they wished, to set up Juvenile Employment Bureaux, this Act laid the foundation for a careers service.

1918   EDUCATION ACT ('The Fisher Act')

The 1918 Act required LEAs to submit schemes of development, when requested by the Board of Education, to ensure that a fully national system of public education was being set up. It abolished the limits set on secondary educational expenditure in 1902, and removed the exemptions to the requirement to attend school between the ages of five and 14. It also abolished the 'half-time' system by which children worked for part of the day and attended school for the remainder. It recommended that school leavers aged 14 to 16 should attend 'continuation' schools for the equivalent of a day a week (this was never implemented). If they wished, LEAs were allowed to set up nursery schools or classes for children below school age, and to provide physical and social educational facilities, such as school camps. All fees for elementary schools were abolished.

1923   EDUCATION ACT (NORTHERN IRELAND) ('The Londonderry Act')

This Act created County and County Borough Education Authorities, and Regional and County Borough Education Committees, in Northern Ireland. They were given powers to ensure adequate elementary and higher education within their areas; and provision was made for existing schools to transfer to these new authorities. These authorities were made responsible for the 'catechetical instruction' of children in elementary schools, according to their parents' denomination. Education was to be funded from both taxes and rates.

1930   EDUCATION ACT (NORTHERN IRELAND)

The 1930 Act gave the Education Minister power to nominate up to a quarter of the membership of Education Committees in Northern Ireland (it being understood that the nominees would be clergymen); regulated the membership of School Management Committees; and required local education authorities to provide Bible instruction in any school if the parents of 10 or more children demanded it.

1944 EDUCATION ACT ('The Butler Act')

The Butler Act replaced almost all previous educational legislation and laid the foundation for the modern education system. It replaced the Board of Education with a Ministry of Education, and gave the Minister at the head of this a creative rather than a merely controlling function, charging him or her with promoting education in England and Wales.

- It abolished the distinction between elementary and higher education, and set up a unified system of free, compulsory schooling from the age of five to 15 (to be raised when practicable to 16). Pupils could receive this education in the LEAs' own schools, in schools maintained by other organisations, or, in certain circumstances (under Section 56 of the Act), 'otherwise' – in effect, at home.

- It extended the concept of education to cover the needs of those above and below school age, and to include the community's needs for culture and recreation. LEAs could provide nursery schools and classes; they could provide or finance holiday classes, camps, play schemes, swimming baths, community centres and recreation facilities; and were given the responsibility (never implemented) to ensure that all young people up to age 18, and not otherwise in education, received part-time further education by attending a 'county college' for the equivalent of one day a week.

- It created a variety of services to support the basic structure of primary and secondary education, e.g. transport, free milk, medical and dental treatment. School meals were to be provided for all children who wanted them (an obligation on LEAs removed by the 1980 Education Act).

- It formulated a relationship between the county and voluntary sectors which has lasted with little change. Voluntary schools were given the choice of becoming 'aided' or 'controlled' schools and provision was made for a few 'special agreement' schools (see Chapter 6). Standards were set to which all school premises had to conform.

- It named the Minister of Education (who became the Secretary of State for Education and Science in 1964) as the arbiter in disputes between LEAs, LEAs and governors, and LEAs and the public. He or she was given considerable powers, and had to be consulted by LEAs over their general development plans and any specific proposals to establish, close or alter schools (this changed under the 1980 Act).

- It set up two Central Advisory Councils for Education (CACE), one for England and one for Wales, to advise the Minister of Education. A number of major reports were produced in this way (see Chapter 3), but no CACE has been constituted since 1967, and later government reports have been issued by committees set up to consider particular issues. (The provision was repealed in 1986.)

- It laid down guidelines for religious instruction. All schools (county and voluntary) must start the day with a corporate act of worship, although parents have the right of withdrawal and LEAs may rule that it is impracticable to assemble all the pupils (e.g. in very large or split-site schools, or where pupils follow many different religions). All schools must also provide religious instruction (the only part of the curriculum prescribed by law, until the 1988 Education Reform Act), and this must be non-denominational except in voluntary schools.
- It required LEAs (in Section 34) to ascertain the needs of children in their areas for special educational treatment, and recommended that they be educated in ordinary schools wherever possible. Ten categories of handicap were established, including the new 'maladjusted'. (These were abolished by the 1981 Education Act.)
- It required every LEA to appoint a chief education officer.
- It removed restrictions on married women teachers.

During the succeeding years, the various provisions of the Act were replaced by later legislation. The Act was finally repealed by the 1996 Education Act.

1946 EDUCATION ACT

This Act specified the responsibilities of LEAs and governors for the maintenance of voluntary schools, and of LEAs in some circumstances for the enlargement of controlled schools. (Replaced by the 1996 Education Act.)

1947 EDUCATION ACT (NORTHERN IRELAND)

Public elementary education in Northern Ireland was abolished by this Act. In its place a unified system of primary, secondary and further education was set up. Education was to be compulsory from five to 15 years of age. Collective worship and religious education were to be compulsory in all county schools. Each local authority was required to estimate the needs of primary, secondary and further education in its area, and to submit plans for meeting them to the ministry. Local authorities were also required to provide books and stationery; to provide facilities for recreation and physical training; and to ascertain which children in their areas required special education, and provide special schools as necessary. The authorities were enabled to grant scholarships, and to give vocational guidance. Medical inspection was made compulsory for all children. Provision was made for the setting up of voluntary schools. Rules were laid down for the management of schools, and the provision of finance by local authorities.

1948 EMPLOYMENT AND TRAINING ACT

The basis for a Youth Employment Service, which subsequently became the Careers Service, was established by this Act.

1948 EDUCATION (MISCELLANEOUS PROVISIONS) ACT

This Act enabled LEAs to recover the costs of providing primary and secondary education for pupils not belonging to their areas (repealed in the 1980 Education Act) and allowed LEAs to provide clothing grants. (Replaced by the 1996 Education Act.)

1953 EDUCATION (MISCELLANEOUS PROVISIONS) ACT

This Act confirmed the powers of LEAs to pay for pupils to attend independent schools, and enabled LEAs to recover the costs of providing further education for students not belonging to their areas. (The latter provision was repealed in the 1980 Education Act, and the extant provisions of the Act replaced by the 1996 Education Act.)

1958 EDUCATION (AMENDMENT) ACT (NORTHERN IRELAND)

Local education authorities in Northern Ireland were required by this Act to set up management committees for further education institutions, with some degree of autonomy, instead of managing them directly.

1962 EDUCATION ACT

The 1962 Act required LEAs in England and Wales to provide grants for all first-degree courses in accordance with national rules and income scales ('mandatory awards'), and allowed them to provide grants for further and postgraduate education ('discretionary awards'). It authorised the Secretary of State to award grants for postgraduate courses and for older students. (These various powers and responsibilities were modified in the 1973 and 1975 Education Acts.) It also set school leaving dates. (Replaced by the 1996 Education Act.)

1963 LONDON GOVERNMENT ACT

Implemented in 1965, this changed the administration of education in the Greater London area by creating the Inner London Education Authority (responsible for the 12 inner London boroughs and the City) and 20 outer London boroughs, each being a separate LEA. The ILEA was unique in that it dealt only with education, whereas all other local authorities had education alongside other local government responsibilities, such as housing, transport and social services. (The 1988 Education Reform Act abolished the ILEA from April 1990.)

1964 EDUCATION ACT

This Act amended the 1944 legislation which had divided schooling between primary and secondary at age 11, by allowing the break to come between the ages of 10 and 12, to cover the development of middle schools. Such schools have to be 'deemed' either primary (normally eight–12) or secondary (normally nine–13) schools for purposes of classification. (Replaced by the 1996 Education Act.)

1965 REMUNERATION OF TEACHERS ACT

Committees for negotiations on teachers' pay were set up by this Act, which also laid down procedures for arbitration where agreement could not be reached. (It was repealed by the 1987 Teachers' Pay and Conditions Act.)

1965 TEACHING COUNCIL (SCOTLAND) ACT

This set up the General Teaching Council for Scotland to deal with the training, registration and professional conduct of Scottish teachers.

1965 CIRCULAR 10/65 ORGANISATION OF SECONDARY EDUCATION

This Circular declared the (Labour) government's objective of ending selection at 11 plus and eliminating separatism in secondary education. It requested LEAs to prepare and submit to the Secretary of State plans for reorganising secondary education on comprehensive lines, and offered guidance as to methods of achieving this. (This circular was withdrawn in 1970 by Circular 10/70, and effectively reinstated in 1974 by Circular 4/74 (DES)/Circular 112/74 (Welsh Office). See also the 1976 and 1979 Education Acts.)

1966 LOCAL GOVERNMENT ACT

This Act introduced the Rate Support Grant, made LEAs (rather than central government) responsible for paying for school meals and milk, and allocated funds (under Section 11) to local authorities for payment of staff employed specifically for the education and welfare of immigrants.

1967 RATE SUPPORT GRANT (POOLING ARRANGEMENTS) REGULATIONS

Under the 1966 Local Government Act, these Regulations provided for the pooling of expenses incurred by LEAs on teacher training, advanced further education, the education of pupils not belonging to the area of any authority, and the training of educational psychologists.

1967 EDUCATION ACT

Existing responsibilities of LEAs (under the direction of the Secretary of State) for controlled schools were extended to apply to middle schools. (Replaced by the 1996 Education Act.)

1968 EDUCATION ACTS

Two Education Acts were passed in 1968. The first tightened the law on changing the character (e.g. to comprehensive) or age range (e.g. to middle school) of schools. The second required the establishment of boards of governors for polytechnics and other LEA-maintained colleges, and the specification of the governors' functions vis-à-vis those of the LEAs and of the colleges' principals. (Replaced by the 1996 Education Act.)

1968 EDUCATION AMENDMENT ACT (NORTHERN IRELAND)

The 'maintained' school in Northern Ireland was created by this Act. It is a special category of voluntary school on whose management committee the education authority is represented, and for whose buildings and equipment the education authority takes financial responsibility.

1969 CHILDREN AND YOUNG PERSONS ACT

Local authorities were given powers and responsibilities for children not receiving proper education, or in need of care and control.

1970 EDUCATION (HANDICAPPED CHILDREN) ACT

Responsibility for the education of severely subnormal children in England and Wales was transferred by this Act from the health authorities to the local education authorities; LEAs were thereafter responsible for all establishments caring for mentally handicapped children.

1970 EDUCATION (EXAMINATIONS) ACT (NORTHERN IRELAND)

This set up an Examinations Council, GCE Board and CSE Board in Northern Ireland.

1970 CIRCULAR 10/70 ORGANISATION OF SECONDARY EDUCATION

This Circular withdrew Circular 10/65, and affirmed the (Conservative) government's intention to allow individual LEAs to determine the shape of secondary education (selective or comprehensive) in their areas. (This was withdrawn, in its turn, in 1974 by Circular 4/74 (DES)/Circular 112/74 (Welsh Office). See also the 1976 and 1979 Education Acts.)

1970 CIRCULAR 18/70 (DES); 108/70 (WELSH OFFICE) PRIMARY AND SECONDARY EDUCATION IN WALES

The responsibility for primary and secondary education (and related school matters) in Wales was transferred from the Secretary of State for Education and Science to the Secretary of State for Wales. The Secretary of State for Education and Science retained responsibility for a number of educational services in Wales, but these have also been transferred subsequently, apart from those concerning the teaching profession.

1970 CHRONICALLY SICK AND DISABLED PERSONS ACT

This Act required new educational buildings to be made accessible to disabled people, unless this was incompatible with the efficient use of resources.

1971 EDUCATION (MILK) ACT

The 1944 Act was amended so that free milk was provided to pupils over the age of seven only if they attended special schools or qualified on medical grounds. (The 1980 Education Act and the 1986 Social Security Act each further restricted the supply of free milk.)

1971 EDUCATION (AMENDMENT) ACT (NORTHERN IRELAND)

This restricted the provision of free milk in Northern Ireland.

1972 LOCAL GOVERNMENT ACT

Implemented in 1974, this Act reduced the number of LEAs in England and Wales from 163 to 104, by creating some new and larger authorities. In the new system there were 39 counties, eight enlarged Welsh counties, 36 metropolitan districts and, as before, 20 outer London boroughs and the Inner London Education Authority (ILEA). It reaffirmed that LEAs must set up education committees and appoint a chief education officer, but the Secretary of State need no longer be consulted about the appointment of the latter. (Relevant parts replaced by the 1996 Education Act.)

1972 RAISING OF THE SCHOOL-LEAVING AGE ORDER

The school-leaving age was raised to 16 (nearly 30 years after this was recommended in the 1944 Education Act).

1973 EDUCATION ACT

Postgraduate education was excluded from eligibility for LEA discretionary grants (it had been eligible under the 1962 Education Act). The Secretary of State was authorised, in some circumstances, to award supplements to LEA mandatory grants.

1973 EDUCATION (WORK EXPERIENCE) ACT

This Act enabled LEAs to arrange for children under school-leaving age to have work experience as part of their education in the last year of compulsory schooling. (Replaced by the 1996 Education Act.)

1973 EMPLOYMENT AND TRAINING ACT

This required LEAs to set up a careers service. It also set up the Manpower Services Commission (MSC) under the Department of Employment. (The MSC was disbanded as a separate organisation in 1988.)

1973 NATIONAL HEALTH SERVICE REORGANISATION ACT

The school health service was transferred from LEAs to area health authorities, but LEAs were required to provide facilities for dental and medical inspection of pupils. (Relevant parts replaced by the 1996 Education Act.)

1974 EDUCATION (MENTALLY HANDICAPPED CHILDREN) (SCOTLAND) ACT

Responsibility for the education of severely mentally handicapped children was transferred from the health authorities to the local education authorities under this Act. (It was similar to the 1970 Education (Handicapped Children) Act for England and Wales.)

1974 CIRCULAR 4/74 (DES)/CIRCULAR 112/74 (WELSH OFFICE) ORGANISATION OF SECONDARY EDUCATION

This Circular withdrew Circular 10/70, and reaffirmed the (Labour) government's objectives of ending selection at 11 plus and creating a unified system of secondary education. It required those LEAs who had not already done so to submit to the Secretaries of State, by the end of the year, information about their plans for making their schools comprehensive. (See also the 1976 and 1979 Education Acts.)

1975 EDUCATION ACT

The provisions of the 1962 Education Act were extended to require LEAs to award mandatory grants to students taking the DipHE, HND and initial teacher training courses, and to authorise the Secretary of State to award grants for adult education courses. (It was repealed by the 1993 Education Act.)

1975 SEX DISCRIMINATION ACT

This Act prohibited sex discrimination in admission to schools, appointment of teachers (with exceptions for single-sex schools) and careers advice, and stipulated that neither girls nor boys should be refused access to 'any courses, facilities or other benefits provided' solely on the grounds of their sex.

1975 DIRECT GRANT GRAMMAR SCHOOLS (CESSATION OF GRANT) REGULATIONS

These Regulations specified how and when direct grants were to be phased out.

1976 RACE RELATIONS ACT

This Act prohibited discrimination on the grounds of race in admission to schools, appointment of teachers, careers advice, access to facilities and the award of discretionary grants. 'Positive discrimination' in favour of disadvantaged racial groups is not normally allowed, e.g. in recruitment or promotion. In some closely defined circumstances, however, where it can be shown that a particular racial group has a special need with regard to education or training, access to facilities may be restricted or allocated first to its members.

1976 EDUCATION ACT

This attempted to abolish selection by ability for secondary schools. It laid down the general principle of comprehensive education which would have ended selection over a period (but this was repealed in the 1979 Act). Added to the main Bill were six miscellaneous sections. One limited the powers of LEAs to pay for places in independent schools, another (Section 10) encouraged the education of handicapped children in ordinary schools. (Replaced by the 1996 Education Act.)

1976 EDUCATION (SCHOOL-LEAVING DATES) ACT

This Act set the date in the summer term after which children aged 16 are no longer required to attend school. (It was repealed by the 1993 Education Act.)

1979 EDUCATION ACT

This repealed the obligation placed on LEAs by the 1976 Education Act to provide plans for comprehensive reorganisation.

1980 EDUCATION ACT

The provisions of this Act were as follows:

- The obligation to provide free school milk and to provide school meals was removed, allowing LEAs to provide milk or meals or not as they wished, at whatever cost or standard they chose (including free milk or meals, if they wished, for families on low incomes), apart from a responsibility to provide free meals for children of families receiving Supplementary Benefit or Family Income Supplement, and to provide facilities free of charge for pupils to eat food brought from home. (These powers and responsibilities were altered in the 1986 Social Security Act.)

- The Assisted Places Scheme was created, whereby pupils can be transferred from maintained to particular independent schools, with the government paying part or all of the tuition fees; the Secretary of State was authorised to establish the details of the scheme by issuing regulations.
- It required all independent schools to be registered, and abolished the previous category of 'recognised as efficient'.
- Parents were given a right to choose the school they wanted their child to go to, although the LEA could refuse on the grounds of inefficient use of resources (and the parents could appeal).
- Parents were given rights to be represented on school governing bodies. LEAs and school governors were required to provide information to parents on such matters as criteria for admission, exam results, curriculum, discipline and organisation. (But see the 1986 Education Act and the 1988 Education Reform Act.)
- It affirmed that provision by LEAs of education for under-fives was discretionary not compulsory.
- Section 13 of the 1944 Act, concerning the establishing, closing or altering of maintained schools by LEAs, was repealed. Now the Secretary of State's approval was required only if there were local objections to a proposal.
- It introduced greater control over the advanced further education pool (known as 'capping').
- The Secretary of State for Wales was authorised to give financial assistance to LEAs for the teaching of Welsh or the use of Welsh as a medium for teaching other subjects.
- It restricted the rights of LEAs to refuse to provide primary, secondary or further education for pupils or students not belonging to their areas, and their powers to recover the costs of providing it.

(Replaced by the 1996 Education Act.)

1980 EDUCATION (SCOTLAND) ACT

A largely consolidating Act, this incorporated measures enacted separately during the 1960s and 1970s, and reaffirmed the legal framework for education in Scotland. It covered all types of school – public (i.e. maintained), grant-aided and independent. It empowered the Secretary of State for Scotland to issue regulations governing the conduct and the responsibilities of local education authorities. In addition, it defined the responsibilities and rights of parents; established the Scottish Examination Board to conduct Scottish Certificate of Education (SCE) examinations; set up committees for negotiating teachers' pay settlements, laying down arbitration procedures where agreement could not be reached; and made provision for children with special educational needs.

1981 EDUCATION ACT

Following the recommendations of the Warnock Report (see Chapter 3, 1978 Warnock), this Act altered the law relating to the education of children with special educational needs. It replaced the previous categories of handicap with the concept of special educational needs, defined as existing where a child has significantly greater difficulty in learning than the majority of children of the same age, or has a disability that prevents or hinders him or her from using the educational facilities normally available. LEAs were given carefully defined responsibilities, to identify the needs of children with a learning difficulty which, in the view of an LEA, calls for it to determine the provision required for the child. The Act set up a detailed assessment procedure for ascertaining these needs, giving parents the right to be consulted, and to appeal against an LEA's decision about appropriate provision. It also reaffirmed, with greater emphasis than the 1944 Act, the principle that children with special educational needs should normally be educated in ordinary schools provided that their needs can be met there, that the education of the other children does not suffer, and that it is compatible with the 'efficient use of resources'. (It was almost entirely repealed by the 1993 Education Act, and what remained was replaced by the 1996 Education Act.)

1981 EDUCATION (SCOTLAND) ACT

This gave parents in Scotland the right to choose which school their children should attend.

1984 EDUCATION (GRANTS AND AWARDS) ACT

This allowed the government to allocate sums of money to LEAs for particular educational purposes, thus reducing the local authorities' control over how the block grant was spent. This reserved money was offered in the form of education support grants (ESGs) of up to 75% of the cost of each project, in areas of education that the Secretary of State had deemed to be important. (Replaced by the 1996 Education Act.)

1986 EDUCATION ACTS

Two Education Acts were passed in 1986 plus an Education (Amendment) Act.

The first of the main Acts made some alterations to the existing arrangements for the pooling of expenditure by LEAs.

The second main Act required every maintained school to have a governing body, and set a formula for the numbers of parent, voluntary body and LEA representatives, which depended on the type and size of the school. Parent representation was strengthened. It required governors to present an annual report to parents at the school, and to arrange a meeting with them to discuss it. It gave governors the responsibility for determining sex education policy in the school, and preventing 'political indoctrination'. Governors were also to 'use their best endeavours' to ensure that children with special educational needs were identified and suitable provision made. Corporal punishment was prohibited in state schools from August 1987; independent schools may still use it, but not on pupils whose fees are paid by the state. This Act also introduced the Local Education Authorities Training Grants Scheme for in-service education of teachers (see Chapter 8). (Replaced by the 1996 Education Act.)

1986 SOCIAL SECURITY ACT

From 1988, the provisions of the 1980 Education Act concerning free school meals and milk were abolished. LEAs no longer have the power to supply free school meals or milk to any children other than those from families receiving Income Support; and they no longer have any obligation to supply free meals or milk to *any* children (even those from families receiving Income Support).

1987 TEACHERS' PAY AND CONDITIONS ACT

This Act abolished the negotiating procedures set up in the 1965 Remuneration of Teachers Act, replacing them until 1990 by authorising the Secretary of State to appoint an interim advisory committee and to impose teachers' pay and conditions. (It was repealed by the 1991 School Teachers' Pay and Conditions Act.)

1988 LOCAL GOVERNMENT ACT

This included an amendment (Section 28) forbidding local authorities to 'promote teaching in any maintained school of the acceptability of homosexuality as a pretended family relationship'. (There is still uncertainty as to whether this section has any practical effect on schools, because of vagueness in the wording of the amendment. See Macnair, 1989.)

1988 EDUCATION REFORM ACT

The main provisions of the Act are as follows:

- It empowered the Secretary of State to prescribe a common curriculum (to be called the national curriculum) for pupils of compulsory school age in maintained schools (for details, see Chapter 10), to set attainment targets for each of its constituent subjects at the ages of seven, 11, 14, and 16, and to make arrangements for assessing how well these are met; established a National Curriculum Council (for England) and a Curriculum Council for Wales to oversee the implementation and assessment of the national curriculum; required LEAs, school governors and headteachers to ensure that the national curriculum is taught in all maintained schools. (These provisions apply to 'grant-maintained' schools (see below). They do not apply to independent schools.)
- It established mechanisms to ensure that the limits set by LEAs or governors on the number of pupils a maintained school admits are not lower than the school is physically capable of accommodating, normally the number admitted in 1979, when school rolls were at their highest. Parents may send their children to any school that has room for them, provided that it caters for their age and aptitude. (These provisions apply to 'grant-maintained' schools (see below).)
- It required LEAs to delegate certain responsibilities for financial management and the appointment and dismissal of staff to the governing bodies of schools; permitted the governing bodies to delegate many of these responsibilities to headteachers (see Chapter 8).
- It allowed a maintained secondary school, or a primary school with over 300 pupils (extended in 1990 to all primary schools), on the resolution of its governing body, with the consent of a majority of those parents who vote in a secret ballot, and with the approval of the Secretary of State, to opt out of LEA finance and control, and be given 'grant-maintained' status. (If fewer than half the parents vote, a second ballot must be held within 14 days. The results of the second ballot will be binding, regardless of how many parents vote in it.) The school will then own its own premises, employ its own staff, and receive an annual grant directly from central government. The character and size of a grant-maintained school cannot be altered, or the premises sold, without the consent of the Secretary of State.
- It empowered the Secretary of State to enter into long-term agreements to fund city technology colleges (see Chapter 5).
- It removed polytechnics and certain other colleges of higher education from LEA control, making them 'free-standing statutory corporations', under the direction of boards of governors whose members are initially appointed by the Secretary of State (see Chapter 5).

- It required LEAs to delegate certain responsibilities for financial management and the appointment and dismissal of staff to the governing bodies of the larger colleges remaining under LEA control.
- It placed the funding of higher education in the hands of two statutory bodies, a Universities Funding Council (UFC) (replacing the University Grants Committee), and a Polytechnics and Colleges Funding Council (PCFC) to administer funds for higher education provided directly by the Secretary of State. The councils had the power to attach terms and conditions to the provision of funds to any institution. Both bodies were independent of government. Their members were to be appointed by the Secretary of State, with between 40% and 60% of the membership to come from higher education.
- It forbade the granting of academic tenure (see Chapter 7) to new university academic staff; withdrew tenure from staff in posts who move to a different university or accept promotion within the same university. At the same time it affirmed that academic staff may not be dismissed for holding particular beliefs or following particular lines of inquiry.
- It abolished the Inner London Education Authority (see Chapter 6) transferring its responsibilities from April 1990 to the inner London boroughs and the City of London.

(Replaced by the 1996 Education Act.)

1988 SCHOOL BOARDS (SCOTLAND) ACT

This established school boards for Scottish schools, with strong parental and community representation. The boards have extensive rights to be informed and consulted about their schools' educational, disciplinary and financial policies and achievements, and to participate in the appointment of senior staff.

1989 SELF-GOVERNING SCHOOLS ETC. (SCOTLAND) ACT

This established procedures whereby Scottish schools could 'opt out' of finance and control by education authorities, and receive funding directly from the Scottish Central Government. (By 1998, just two schools had done so.)

1989 EDUCATION REFORM (NORTHERN IRELAND) ORDER

By this Order, Northern Ireland follows the main thrust of the English and Welsh reforms. There is a similar, though not identical, common curriculum and pattern of assessment, and a comparable scheme for delegation of financial management to the governing bodies of schools. 'Opting out' is also permitted, but only where a school seeks 'grant-maintained *integrated* status' and chooses to progress towards full integration of Protestant and Roman Catholic pupils.

1990 EDUCATION (STUDENT LOANS) ACT

This Act empowered the respective Secretaries of State to issue regulations making arrangements for students in higher education in England, Wales and Scotland to receive, and repay, loans towards their maintenance. (For details of the arrangements currently in force, see Chapter 8, p. 141.)

1991 SCHOOL TEACHERS' PAY AND CONDITIONS ACT

A review body was established, its members appointed by the government, to make recommendations to the Secretary of State for Education about teachers' salaries and conditions of employment. Final decisions are then made by the Secretary of State, after consultation with LEAs, teachers' representatives and other interested parties, and set out in a School Teachers' Pay and Conditions Document. (The 1987 Teachers' Pay and Conditions Act was repealed.)

1992 TRANSFER OF FUNCTIONS (NATIONAL HERITAGE) ORDER AND TRANSFER OF FUNCTIONS (SCIENCE) ORDER

Responsibility for sport and recreation in England was transferred from the Department of Education and Science to the Department of National Heritage, and for science in England to the Cabinet Office. The Department of Education and Science was renamed the Department for Education.

1992 FURTHER AND HIGHER EDUCATION ACT

Further education colleges became corporations independent of local education authorities, funded by central government largely through two new Further Education Funding Councils (FEFC), one for England, the other for Wales. Sixth-form colleges were removed from LEAs' control, and joined the further education sector as colleges, funded through the FEFCs.

The funding of higher education (universities, polytechnics and other colleges of higher education) was unified. The Universities Funding Council and the Polytechnics and Colleges Funding Council were replaced by two unitary

Higher Education Funding Councils (HEFC), one for England, the other for Wales. All institutions of higher education now have to compete for funding for both teaching and research.

(Although the funding of further education colleges is now largely through the FEFCs, and of universities through the HEFCs, it is the HEFCs that fund any higher education courses in further education colleges, and the FEFCs that fund any further education provision in universities.)

The Council for National Academic Awards, which had validated the degrees of institutions of higher education other than universities, was dissolved. Subject to the approval of the Privy Council in each case, polytechnics and other institutions of higher education may become degree-awarding bodies in their own right and, if they meet certain criteria, may take the title of university. Colleges of higher education that are not permitted to award degrees in their own right may have their degrees validated by a university. [All the polytechnics and two colleges of higher education have adopted the title of university.] (Replaced by the 1996 Education Act.)

1992 FURTHER AND HIGHER EDUCATION (SCOTLAND) ACT

This Act reformed further and higher education in Scotland along lines very similar to those of the 1992 Further and Higher Education Act (for England and Wales). Responsibility for providing further education was transferred from education authorities to the Secretary of State, who was required to make funds available for further education, and authorised to establish a Scottish Further Education Funding Council to assist him or her in allocating these funds. [No such Funding Council has as yet been established.] Colleges of further education are to be managed by new Boards of Management, corporate bodies independent of education authorities and subject to the direction of the Secretary of State. The funding of higher education was unified, with the establishment of a Higher Education Funding Council for Scotland, taking over the functions of the Universities Funding Council in Scotland (for universities) and the Scottish Office Education Department (for other institutions of higher education). Subject to their meeting certain criteria, all institutions of higher education could take the title of university. [Five had done so by the end of 1993, giving Scotland 12 universities in all.]

1992 EDUCATION (SCHOOLS) ACT

This Act and the Education (Schools Inspection) Regulations 1993 issued under it establish new arrangements for the inspection of schools. Inspection of schools is to be the responsibility in England of what became known as the Office for Standards in Education (OFSTED), a non-ministerial department, independent of the DFE, headed by Her Majesty's Chief Inspector of Schools; and in Wales of the Office of Her Majesty's Chief Inspector of Schools in Wales (OHMCI Wales), similarly independent of the Education Department of the Welsh Office. OFSTED and OHMCI are to identify, train and register a suitable body of *Registered Inspectors* and *Independent Inspectors*, not in the employ of OFSTED or OHMCI. Actual inspections of schools and colleges will now normally be conducted by teams of these Independent Inspectors, headed by a Registered Inspector, and including at least one *Lay Inspector* who has not been involved professionally in education. A team will be offered a contract by OFSTED or OHMCI for the inspection of a school or college, after it has invited tenders from at least two Registered Inspectors. Every maintained school (including grant-maintained schools and CTCs) and some independent schools (notably those catering for children with special educational needs) is to have a four-yearly inspection, lasting not more than two weeks, and normally not more than one. The inspectors must report on the quality of education provided, the educational standards achieved, the efficiency of financial management and the 'spiritual, moral, social and cultural development' of the pupils. Her Majesty's Inspectors of Schools (HMIs), who traditionally conducted school inspections, will now have a more organisational, administrative, training and supervisory role. (Replaced by the 1996 Education Act and the 1996 School Inspections Act.)

1993 EDUCATION ACT

This Act contains a number of miscellaneous provisions.

New provisions are made for grant-maintained schools. They are to be financed in England through the Funding Agency for Schools (FAS), whose members are to be chosen by the Secretary of State for Education, who is empowered to issue directives to it. (A parallel body may be established for Wales if numbers of GM schools there justify this.) In addition to being responsible for the funding of grant-maintained schools, the FAS may in time assume all or part of the responsibilities currently held by local education authorities for planning the provision of education in their areas. When the percentage of the primary or secondary pupils in an LEA's area who attend grant-maintained schools reaches 10%, the Secretary of State is empowered to transfer part of these responsibilities; when it reaches 75%, he or she is empowered to transfer all the responsibilities. The process for LEA-maintained schools to become grant-maintained by 'opting out' of LEA control is simplified. And other ways of establishing grant-maintained schools are introduced. Independent schools may 'opt in' to grant-maintained status, or entirely new schools may be set up within the grant-maintained sector, on the initiative of the Funding Agency or of local 'promoters'.

Methods are introduced of dealing with schools identified as unsatisfactory by school inspectors. In the first instance, the LEA may appoint new governors, and withdraw delegated management from such a school. If the school continues to be judged unsatisfactory, central government may put it under the management of an appointed Educational Association, centrally financed, until its performance is judged acceptable.

Pupils excluded from schools must now be excluded either permanently or for a fixed term not exceeding 15 school days in any one term; the category of indefinite exclusion is abolished. LEAs must provide education for excluded pupils in Pupil Referral Units, which must offer a broad and balanced curriculum, but need not offer the full national curriculum.

In addition, the National Curriculum Council and the School Examinations and Assessment Council are replaced by a unitary School Curriculum and Assessment Authority. Parents are permitted to remove their children from sex education lessons. The provision of religious education is extended. The Secretary of State is empowered to issue regulations and a code of practice concerning the education of children with special educational needs. Finally the regulations governing the allocation of school places are modified. (Replaced by the 1996 Education Act and the 1996 School Inspections Act.)

1994 EDUCATION ACT

This Act deals with two separate topics, teacher training in England and Wales, and students' unions in England, Wales and Scotland.

The Act establishes a Teacher Training Agency for England and Wales. Its membership is decided by the Secretary of State, who has regard to the desirability of including persons with successful experience of teaching, teacher training, the provision of education, and industrial, commercial or financial matters or the practice of any profession. The Agency provides information and advice on teaching as a career, and acts in England as the funding agency for teacher training courses and related activities which the governing bodies of eligible institutions consider necessary or desirable. (The funding agency for teacher training in Wales is the Higher Education Funding Council for Wales.) Institutions eligible for funding include all institutions of higher or further education, all schools, and any partnerships between eligible institutions. The objectives of the Agency include securing the involvement of schools in all courses for the initial and in-service training of teachers, and establishing 'an appropriate balance' between courses provided wholly or mainly by schools and other courses. The terms and conditions under which grants are made by the Agency must not refer to the content of particular courses of study or research programmes, or the way in which they are taught, supervised or assessed.

The Act also regulates the conduct of students' unions in England, Wales and Scotland, in establishments of higher or further education, funded by the appropriate Higher or Further Education Funding Councils or the Scottish Office. The governing bodies of such establishments must ensure that students' unions operate in a fair and democratic manner, and are accountable for their finances. Any student must have the right not to be a member of a union or to be represented by it, without thereby being unfairly disadvantaged in any way, including the provision of services. Appointment to major union offices must be by election in a secret ballot in which all members are entitled to vote. No person should hold sabbatical office or paid elected office in any union for more than two years. Allocation of resources by the union to groups or clubs must be fair and open. Affiliation of the union to any external organisation must be open, and subject to at least annual review by the members.

1996 EDUCATION (STUDENT LOANS) ACT

A brief act, authorising payment of subsidies to banks, building societies and other private sector organisations to enable them to make loans to students in higher education similar to the public sector loans made by the Student Loans Company. (It amends the 1990 act of the same title.)

1996 EDUCATION (SCOTLAND) ACT

(1) The Scottish Qualifications Authority (SQA) is established, replacing the Scottish Examination Board and the Scottish Vocational Education Council. (2) Statutory form, nationwide, is given to the nursery voucher scheme already piloted in certain areas. [A voucher, initially worth £1,100, was to be given to parents of every eligible child, who could use it towards the purchase of nursery education from any approved supplier, public, private or voluntary. This scheme was withdrawn by the new Labour Government.] (3) Regulations concerning membership of and elections to School Boards are amended. (4) A number of miscellaneous provisions are enacted, including: arrangements for the assessment and testing of pupils in the first two years of secondary school, under the auspices of the new SQA; provision for the reservation of places at popular schools for pupils who may move into their catchment area during a school year.

1996 NURSERY EDUCATION AND GRANT-MAINTAINED SCHOOLS ACT

(1) The Secretary of State is empowered to make grants to LEAs and other providers of nursery education. In effect, this authorises the 'voucher' scheme, though the word does not appear in the act. [A voucher, initially worth £1,100, was to be given to parents of every eligible child, who could use it towards the

purchase of nursery education from any approved supplier, public, private or voluntary. This scheme was withdrawn by the new Labour Government.] (2) Governing bodies of grant-maintained schools are permitted to borrow money and offer security.

1996 EDUCATION ACT

A huge act, but almost entirely concerned to consolidate existing laws, with little or no change to their effect: 18 complete acts currently in force and substantial parts of other acts are repealed and in effect re-enacted. (The last surviving parts of the 1944 Education Act are finally repealed.)

1996 SCHOOL INSPECTIONS ACT

This act consolidates previous legislation concerning school inspection (mainly the 1992 Education (Schools) Act and parts of the 1993 Education Act), with little or no change to its effect.

1997 EDUCATION ACT

The last education act introduced by the Conservative Government, its final form was a compromise with the Labour Opposition in which controversial clauses (mainly about the establishment of new grant-maintained schools, and the right of schools to select pupils) were removed to allow the act to be passed. Its main provisions now concern school discipline. Schools may make admission conditional on parents' signing a home-school agreement accepting certain responsibilities. Detention outside school hours may be imposed on pupils without their parents' consent. Schools' right to exclude pupils for 15 days per term is amended to 45 days per year, and arrangements for appeal against exclusion are established. The powers of teachers to restrain pupils physically are defined. In addition, there are a number of miscellaneous provisions. These include the establishment (for England) of the Qualifications and Curriculum Authority (QCA) to replace the School Curriculum and Assessment Authority and the National Council for Vocational Qualifications, and the definition of its functions; and the renaming of the Curriculum and Assessment Authority for Wales as the Qualifications, Curriculum and Assessment Authority for Wales, and the definition of its functions. Arrangements are also made for home-school partnership documents, for baseline assessment schemes, for school performance targets and for careers education in school. [The Act also provided for the extension of the Assisted Places Scheme to schools providing primary education only; however, the entire Scheme was abolished soon after under the new Labour Government.]

1997 EDUCATION (SCHOOLS) ACT

The first education act introduced by the Labour Government, this abolished the Assisted Places Scheme in England, Wales and Scotland, with transitional arrangements to protect the interests of currently assisted pupils.

1998 EDUCATION (STUDENT LOANS) ACT

This makes arrangements for the transfer of public sector student loans to the private sector. (It amends the 1990 act of the same title.)

1998 SCHOOL STANDARDS AND FRAMEWORK ACT

(1) Limits are placed on infant class sizes, and grants may be paid to LEAs to enable them to meet these. (2) The responsibilities of LEAs are defined, and the Secretary of State given powers to ensure that they fulfil them adequately. (3) Powers are defined for both LEAs and the Secretary of State to intervene in schools judged unsatisfactory. (4) Arrangements are made to establish Education Action Zones, where clusters of schools will work together, assume some of the LEA's functions, and receive government grants. (5) A new framework for schools is defined, to be implemented from 2000, with the categories of: community (replacing county), foundation (replacing grant-maintained), voluntary (aided or controlled, as before), community special and foundation special schools. Procedures are established by which schools will be assigned to their new category. A number of provisions consequent on the establishment of this new framework are also included, such as provision for establishing and closing schools and for admitting pupils, and the dissolution of the Funding Agency for Schools.

1998 TEACHING AND HIGHER EDUCATION ACT

(1) A General Teaching Council for England and Wales is established from 2000 (with provision for separate bodies for the two countries later). Teachers will have to be registered by the Council. (2) A compulsory qualification is to be required for new headteachers. (3) The functions of OFSTED in inspecting initial teacher training are clarified. (4) The present combination of loans and grants for student maintenance is replaced by one of enhanced loans only, and students are also required to pay means-tested contributions to their tuition fees of up to £1,000 per annum.

1998 GOVERNMENT OF WALES ACT

This establishes the National Assembly for Wales (Cynulliad Cenedlaethol Cymru), with the first elections having taken place in May 1999. It has powers to enact secondary legislation within its areas of responsibility, which include education. The executive functions relating to education formerly performed by ministers of the UK Welsh Office have been transferred to ministers responsible to the Assembly.

1998 NORTHERN IRELAND ACT

This establishes the Northern Ireland Assembly, which is to have full powers to enact, repeal and amend legislation within its areas of responsibility, including education. The executive functions relating to education formerly performed by ministers of the UK Northern Ireland Office are to be transferred to ministers responsible to the Assembly. [However, as we go to press in early 1999, the future of devolved government in Northern Ireland is uncertain, as negotiations continue between the UK Government and the Northern Ireland political parties over the decommissioning of weapons held by paramilitary organizations.]

1998 SCOTLAND ACT

This establishes the Scottish Parliament, the first elections having taken place in May 1999. It has full powers to enact, repeal and amend legislation within its areas of responsibility, which include education. The executive functions relating to education formerly performed by ministers of the UK Scottish Office have been transferred to ministers responsible to the Scottish Parliament.

SOURCES AND FURTHER READING

The standard reference work on educational law in England and Wales is – in its ninth edition – Liell et al (1995). It is not frozen at its date of publication, however, but is produced in loose-leaf form, and kept up to date with additional pages to cover new developments, and with frequent supplementary bulletins giving news about the progress of laws through Parliament, the issue of ministerial orders and regulations under various acts, court cases and other developments relevant to educational law. The texts of statutes and statutory instruments are printed in full. These do not make easy reading for those untrained in law, but they are interspersed with explanatory comments that are accessible and useful to the lay reader.

By contrast, the Croner guides – also issued in loose-leaf form and updated – are designed for readers who have not studied law.

Croner (no single date) *The Head's Legal Guide*, Kingston-upon-Thames: Croner Publications Ltd.

Croner (no single date) *The Teacher's Legal Guide*, Kingston-upon-Thames: Croner Publications Ltd.

Hyndman, M. (1978) *Schools and Schooling in England and Wales: A Documentary History*, London: Harper and Row.

Le Métais, J. (1995) *Legislating for Change: School Reforms in England and Wales 1979–1994*, Slough: NFER.

Liell, P., Coleman, J. E. and Poole, K. P. (1995 but with later additions and bulletins) *The Law of Education*, 9th edn, London: Butterworth.

Maclure S. (ed.) (1986) *Educational Documents, England and Wales, 1816 to the Present Day*, London: Methuen.

Maclure, S. (1989) *Education Re-formed: a guide to the Education Reform Act*, 2nd edn, London: Hodder and Stoughton.

Macnair, M. R. T. (1989) Homosexuality in schools – Section 28, Local Government Act 1988, *Education and the Law*, Vol. 1, No. 1, pp. 35–9.

This chapter describes, with some basic facts and figures, the range of institutions that make up the United Kingdom's education system.

> **FACT** The United Kingdom has just under 34,000 schools in total (31,000 in the maintained sector), with 454,000 teachers and over 9.8 million pupils (1995–6 figures: GSS, 1997, Tables 2, 11 and 12).

(A) PRESCHOOL

Preschool provision by an LEA may take the form of:

- *Nursery schools* – Separate schools for 2–5-year-olds, each with its own headteacher and a number of classes staffed by teachers and nursery assistants who have trained under the National Nursery Examination Board (NNEB). The recommended child/adult ratio is 13 to 1 (or 22 to 1 if qualified teachers only are counted).
- *Nursery classes within primary schools* – Separate classes for 3–5-year-olds which are an integral part of a primary school, with staffing as for nursery schools.
- *Reception classes* – Children who are just under compulsory school age can gain early admission to the first (reception) class in an infant or first school.

There is no obligation on LEAs to provide preschool education (except for children identified as having special educational needs) and provision varies greatly, both in amount and in type. In Wales, 73% of 3- and 4-year-old children go to maintained nursery or primary schools, full- or part-time, compared with 54% in England, 46% in Northern Ireland and 36% in Scotland (ONS, 1997, Table 4.4: 1995–6 figures). The percentage of 3- and 4-year-olds attending school has risen substantially in recent years, but substantial variation in amount and type of provision is still found between regions, and between individual LEAs. (This is illustrated for England in Figures 5.1, 5.2 and 5.3.)

Preschool children may also attend *day nurseries* provided by local authority Social Services Departments for children in need. Private provision, including *playgroups*, *day nurseries* and *childminders*, has to be registered with local authority Social Services Departments. In 1993, in the United Kingdom, some 28,000 children attended local authority day nurseries, 127,000 attended other registered day nurseries, 352,000 went to registered childminders and another

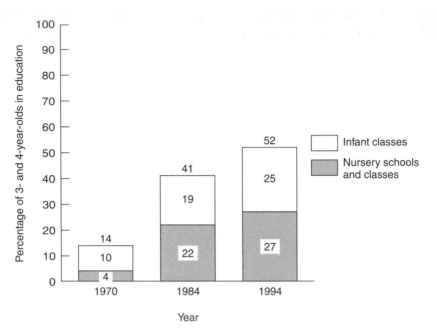

Figure 5.1   *Percentage of 3- and 4-year-olds in full- or part-time maintained education,*
England 1970–94
(Adapted from DFE, 1994, Table 1; DFE, 1995, Table 1)

475,000 went to registered playgroups (CSO, 1995, Table 3.3). Figure 5.4 shows how these forms of provision have changed over time.

There are also *independent schools* that cater for preschool children. There are two main types: those that are basically preparatory schools – preparing very young children for entry to a highly academic independent school later on

> **F A C T**   In the United Kingdom in 1995–6, there were 1,490 publicly maintained nursery schools catering for some 84,000 children. But the majority of under-fives received their education in primary schools, 366,000 in nursery classes, and 621,000 in reception classes. Another 67,000 under-fives went to private schools, and 8,000 to special schools. Altogether just over 70% of the 3- and 4-year-old population received some education at school, mostly on a part-time basis (GSS, 1997, Tables 1, 2 and 13b).

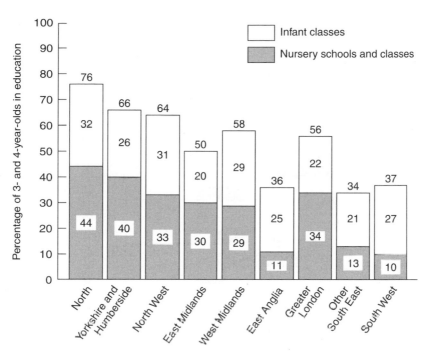

*Figure 5.2   Percentage of 3- and 4-year-olds in full- or part-time maintained education,
England 1994: regional variations
(Adapted from DFE, 1995, Table 2)
Note: The regions here are the older Standard Statistical Regions, not the newer
Government Office Regions. (See Chapter 2 above)*

– and those that are a fee-paying alternative to maintained nursery schools,
either because preschool places are in short supply or because the school
adopts a particular educational philosophy, such as the Montessori method.
Since 1979, they too have been required to register with local authority Social
Services Departments, and are not counted in the official education statistics.

Some common patterns of early childhood experience are shown in Figure
5.5.

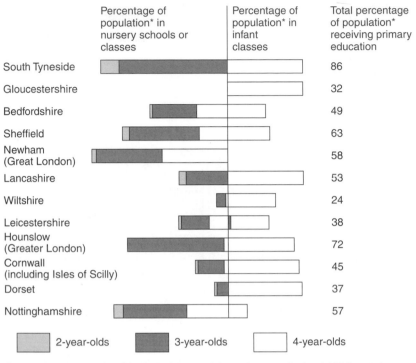

	Percentage of population* in nursery schools or classes	Percentage of population* in infant classes	Total percentage of population* receiving primary education
South Tyneside			86
Gloucestershire			32
Bedfordshire			49
Sheffield			63
Newham (Great London)			58
Lancashire			53
Wiltshire			24
Leicestershire			38
Hounslow (Greater London)			72
Cornwall (including Isles of Scilly)			45
Dorset			37
Nottinghamshire			57

2-year-olds   3-year-olds   4-year-olds

*Figure 5.3   Percentage of 2-, 3- and 4-year-olds in education, England 1994; variations among selected LEAs (*Expressed as a percentage of the estimated total population of 3- and 4-year-olds)*
(Adapted from DFE, 1995, Table 3)
Note: Any category with a percentage figure of less than 1 is omitted from the diagram. Full-time and part-time pupils are combined

(B) PRIMARY

The usual definition of primary education covers children aged 5–11 years in England and Wales, 4–11 years in Northern Ireland, and 5–12 years in Scotland. Primary schools consist mainly of:

- *Infants schools* – for children aged 5–7 years.
- *Junior schools* – for those aged 7–11 years.
- *Combined junior and infants schools* – these are the most common and cater for children of both age groups.

An alternative system, introduced in some areas in the late 1960s, is the three-tier system, of *lower* (or *first*), *middle* and *upper schools*, based on the idea that

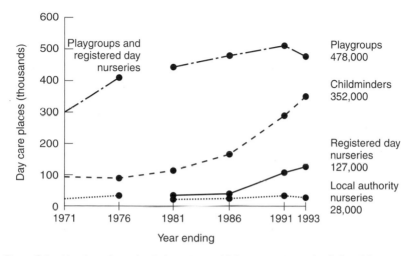

Figure 5.4 *Number of preschool places in establishments registered with Social Services Departments (i.e. forms of preschool provision that are not part of the education system), United Kingdom 1966–92*
(Adapted from CSO, 1994, Table 3.3)
Note: Local authority nurseries include local authority playgroups up to 1976

the age of 8, 9 or even 10 was a more appropriate time for children to make the transition between the informal teaching of the early years and the more formal subject teaching offered later.

Middle schools developed in a variety of patterns; some catered for 8–12-year-olds (deemed primary), others for 9–13-year-olds (deemed primary or secondary at the discretion of the LEA) and yet others for 10–14-year-olds (deemed secondary). Middle schools are confined almost entirely to England;

	0 year	1 year	2 years	3 years	4 years	5 years	6 years
Child 1	Childminder or day nursery			Nursery class		Primary class	
Child 2	Home		Nursery school			Primary class	
Child 3	Home		Nursery class		Primary class		
Child 4	Home			Playgroup		Primary class	
Child 5	Home					Primary class	
Child 6	Combined nursery centre					Primary class	
Child 7	Home			Private nursery		Preparatory school class	

Figure 5.5 *Some common patterns of early childhood experience*

Wales has just one, and Scotland, which never had more than two, now has none.

> **F A C T**   In the United Kingdom in 1994–5, there were 23,500 maintained primary schools, including about 500 middle schools deemed primary. Virtually all were mixed-sex schools. Between them they taught 5.2 million children and employed 225,900 teachers (83% female) (GSS, 1997, Tables 11, 15 and 16).

Size of schools

In 1995–6, over threequarters of maintained primary school pupils in the United Kingdom attended a school with more than 200 pupils. Almost all the rest attended a school with between 50 and 200. Very small schools, with under 50 pupils accounted for only 1% of primary pupils in the UK (but 3% of those in Scotland and in Wales, and 2% of those in Northern Ireland) (ONS, 1997, Table 4.3).

School closures and falling rolls

Between 1980 and 1996, more than 3,300 maintained primary schools closed in the United Kingdom (see Figure 5.6).

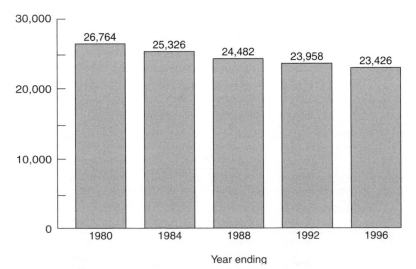

Figure 5.6   Numbers of maintained primary schools, United Kingdom 1980–96 (Adapted from GSS, 1983, 1985, 1989, 1994 and 1997, Table 2)

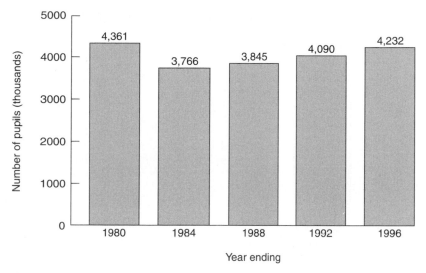

Figure 5.7   Primary school rolls, England 1980–96 (maintained schools, full- and part-time pupils)
(Adapted from DES, 1989, Table 1; GSS, 1994, Table 15; ONS, 1997, Table 4.1)

These closures have to be seen in the context of changes in the number of children at primary school; this is illustrated in Figure 5.7, using data for England.

Pupil/teacher ratios

Pupil/teacher ratios in primary schools fell during the 1970s and 1980s (especially the 1970s) but rose again in the 1990s. This is illustrated in Figure 5.8.

The pupil/teacher ratio in maintained primary schools varies from country to country. Compared with the United Kingdom average of 22.7 to 1, it is rather higher in England (23.2) and lower in Wales (22.5), Northern Ireland (20.4) and Scotland (19.5) (ONS, 1997, Table 4.1: 1995–6 figures. See also Chapter 8 below, Part 2, p. 149).

(C) SECONDARY

Secondary education is compulsory up to the age of 16, and pupils can stay on at school for up to three years longer.

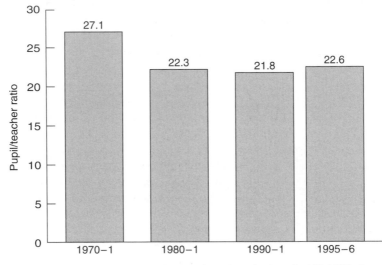

Figure 5.8   Pupil/teacher ratios in maintained primary schools in the UK, 1970–1 to 1995–6
(Adapted from GSS, 1994, Table 14; ONS, 1998, Table 5.3

F A C T   In the United Kingdom in 1995–6, there were nearly 4,500 maintained secondary schools, of which 15% were grant maintained. Between them they taught 3.7 million children and employed 228,000 teachers (51% female) (ONS, 1998, Tables 5.3 and 5.9).

The following list of types of secondary schools includes some that now exist only in very small numbers, often in just a few LEAs.

Tripartite system

Grammar, secondary modern and technical schools in England and Wales (and, with different terminology, in Scotland and Northern Ireland – see below) form what is called the tripartite system, though in reality, technical schools have never existed in large numbers. The tripartite system now forms a very small and highly localised part of secondary schooling in Great Britain, where maintained secondary education became almost entirely comprehensive during the 1980s and 1990s (see Figure 5.9). The principal characteristics of tripartite schools are as follows:

- *Grammar schools* provide a mainly academic education for pupils aged 11 to 19 who have been selected on the basis of ability.
- *Secondary modern schools* provide a general education for those who do not go to grammar schools, usually up to the minimum school-leaving age (though pupils can stay on longer).
- *Technical schools* provide a general education but with considerable emphasis on technical subjects. These never existed in large numbers and are now almost extinct: by the 1990s, only four remained in England and none in Scotland, Wales or Northern Ireland (GSS, 1994, Table 18).

In Scotland, the closest equivalent to English and Welsh grammar schools were called *senior secondary schools*, while the equivalents of secondary moderns were *junior secondary schools*. (However, the phrase 'grammar school' does sometimes appear in the names of particular schools in Scotland.)

In Northern Ireland, a selective system still predominates, though with a few comprehensive schools in certain areas. In 1996–7, 41% of secondary pupils attended grammar schools and 59% attended *secondary intermediate* (or simply 'secondary') schools – the Northern Ireland equivalent of England's secondary

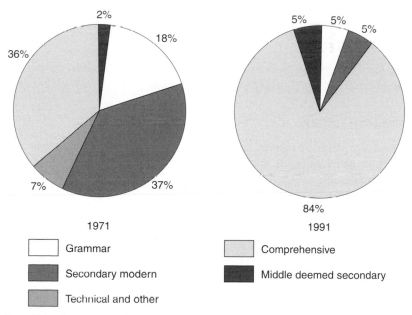

Figure 5.9   *Percentages of pupils in different kinds of maintained secondary schools, United Kingdom 1971 and 1991*
(Adapted from GSS, 1989 and 1994, Table 18)

modern schools. (Until the 1970s, Northern Ireland also had technical schools, but none exist now.) (NISRA, 1998, Table 5.5)

Comprehensive schools

Comprehensive schools take all pupils (except those attending special schools) regardless of ability. There is a great variety of schemes and great variation in the degree to which schools are fully comprehensive: if some schools in an area take the children who are thought to have greater academic ability, the remaining schools, even if called comprehensive, cannot be considered fully so.

Secondary schools with sixth form

These cater for the full age range from 11 (or following middle schools from 12, 13 or 14) to 18 or 19 years.

Secondary schools without sixth form

These cater only for children up to the age of 16. Those pupils wishing to continue their education have either to transfer to a school which does have a sixth form, or to move outside the secondary school system into a sixth form college, tertiary college or other further education college (see below).

Sixth form colleges

Sixth form colleges were moved in 1992 from the schools sector to the further education sector (see below).

Community schools

These are maintained schools which provide education for school pupils and mature students alongside social, recreational and cultural activities for the whole community.

City technology colleges

These have been set up by private sponsors, with government grants to provide a free education with a technological emphasis for 11–18-year-olds. The school day and terms are longer than the legal requirement for state schools. City technology colleges (CTCs) are independent of LEAs: the DfEE pays running costs but promoters own or lease the premises and are responsible for their management, employing teachers, etc. They are required to 'have regard' for the national curriculum. They have not become a substantial part of the secondary system: by 1998, only 15 CTCs had opened.

Technology colleges and other specialist schools

Not to be confused with 'city technology colleges' (see above), technology colleges are state secondary schools which have been given special status and extra public funding, as well as business sponsorship, to place special emphasis on technology, science and mathematics within the full national curriculum. By September 1998, there were 227 technology colleges in England. Similar specialist schools have also been established with other emphases, though they are much fewer: language colleges (58), sports colleges (26) and arts colleges (19).

Size of schools

Secondary schools are generally much larger than primary schools. In 1995–6, 52% of maintained secondary school pupils in the United Kingdom attended a school with between 400 and 1,000 pupils. Another 44% attended a school with more than 1,000 pupils. Smaller schools, with under 400 pupils, accounted for less than 4% of secondary pupils in Britain, but almost 10% of those in Northern Ireland (ONS, 1997, Table 4.3).

School closures and falling rolls

Between 1980 and 1996, over 900 secondary schools closed in the United Kingdom (see Figure 5.10).

These closures have to be seen in the context of changes in the number of children in secondary schools during this period. As Figure 5.11 illustrates, using data for England, the numbers have declined significantly, though not steadily.

Pupil/teacher ratios

Pupil/teacher ratios fell during the 1970s and 1980s, but rose again during the 1990s; this is illustrated in Figure 5.12. The PTR in maintained secondary schools in the United Kingdom was 16.1 to 1 in 1995–6, but there are variations from country to country. The PTR in England is highest (16.6 to 1); in Northern Ireland it is 14.7 to 1; and in Scotland 12.9 to 1 (ONS, 1997, Table 1).

(D) SPECIAL

Special schools provide education for children with special needs, on the grounds that they cannot be educated satisfactorily in an ordinary school. They are generally much smaller than mainstream schools: about 80% of special schools in the United Kingdom have 100 pupils or fewer; 99% have 200 or

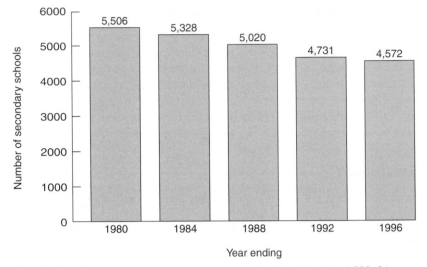

Figure 5.10   Numbers of maintained secondary schools, United Kingdom 1980–96
(Adapted from GSS, 1983, 1985, 1989 and 1994, Table 2; ONS, 1997, Table 5.1)
Note: The 1996 figure includes the 110 sixth form colleges, though they are no longer
officially classified as schools, for consistency with the earlier years

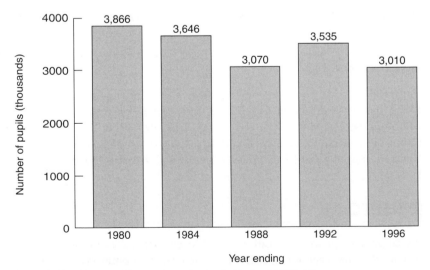

Figure 5.11   Maintained secondary school rolls, England 1980–96
(Adapted from DES, 1989, Table 1 and GSS, 1994, Table 15; ONS, 1997, Table 4.1)

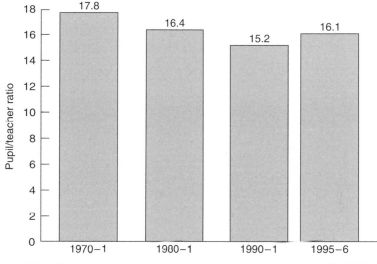

Figure 5.12   Pupil/teacher ratios in maintained secondary schools in the UK, 1970–1 to 1995–6
(Adapted from GSS, 1994, Table 14; ONS, 1998, Table 5.3)

fewer. Special schools often take the full age range, including nursery and post-16. They have a lower pupil/teacher ratio than any other type of school: 6.2 to 1 in the United Kingdom (GSS, 1994, Tables 14 and 15; ONS, 1997, Table 4.1).

> **FACT**   In 1995–6 there were 1,527 special schools or departments in the United Kingdom, including 28 hospital schools and 78 assisted independent schools, with 18,000 teachers and 113,000 pupils. About 88% of them were day schools and the remainder boarding (ONS, 1997, Table 4.1; ONS, 1998, Table 5.1).

Special classes and units may also be provided in mainstream schools (especially primary) for children with particular needs, e.g. the partially hearing or partially sighted, 'disruptive' children or slow learners.

The percentages of children with different types of handicap in special schools are shown in Figure 5.13 for England in 1982 – the last year for which such data were collected. Since the 1981 Education Act (see Chapter 4) came into force in 1983, children assessed as having special educational needs are given an individual 'statement' ('record' in Scotland) of these needs instead of being assigned to a category of handicap (see Chapter 3, 1978 Warnock). In

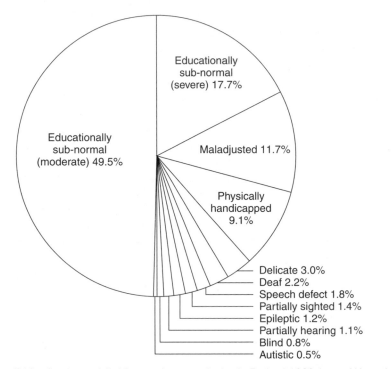

Figure 5.13   Pupils, aged 5–15, attending special schools, England 1982, by pre-Warnock categories of handicap
(Adapted from DES, 1986)

1995–6, 259,000 children in the UK had statements or records of special educational needs – 2.7% of the total school population. Of these children, 58% are in mainstream schooling, and 42% in special schools or departments. This contrasts with the position ten years earlier, when 23% of children with statements of special educational needs were in mainstream schooling, and 78% in special schools or departments (ONS, 1998, Table 5.4).

Since the 1981 Act, the percentage of the total UK school population in special schools has fallen – from 1.4% in 1980–1 to 1.1% in 1995–6 (GSS, 1989, Table 1.4; ONS, 1998, Tables 5.2 and 5.4).

(See Chapter 11 for more facts and figures on special education in relation to sex and ethnic group.)

(E) INDEPENDENT

Independent schools are those outside the maintained education system. They are not funded by the government or local authorities, and most charge fees (see Chapter 11), though a few are wholly charitable institutions. All independent schools have to register with their LEAs (or with the local authority Social Services Department in the case of independent nursery schools) and they can be inspected by OFSTED.

Many independent schools provide a highly academic mainstream education for pupils selected on the basis of ability (usually through an entrance examination), but some are based on alternative philosophies of education, and others offer specialised provision: for example, for the musically gifted, for children with special needs, for children of foreign nationals, or for religious minorities. Independent schools generally have a relatively low pupil/teacher ratio – 10.3 to 1 in 1995–6, compared with 18.0 to 1 in all schools (combined figures for primary and secondary schools) (ONS, 1997, Table 4.1). About a quarter of pupils at independent schools are boarders, a much higher proportion than in maintained schools. Boarding is still common in the well-known public schools, but is declining very rapidly. Public schools normally take children from the age of 13 (usually the boys' boarding schools) or from the age of 11.

Independent schools are also referred to as public schools, private schools, preparatory schools and non-maintained schools. The terms are used loosely and sometimes interchangeably, but the most common meanings appear to be as follows.

Public schools

Especially in England, this term traditionally refers to independent fee-charging, but non-profit-making, secondary schools belonging to various highly prestigious associations. However, many of these now prefer the term 'independent schools', as in the title of the Independent Schools Information Service (ISIS). Associations about which ISIS collects and distributes information include the following. (The figures are for 1999.)

- *Headmasters' Conference (HMC)* – The most prestigious of associations of independent schools including 242 schools, with some 167,000 pupils in total, 75% of whom are boys. Twenty-three per cent of HMC school pupils are full or weekly boarders. Within the HMC, there are smaller and more informal groups of schools, whose headmasters and senior masters meet several times a year to discuss matters of common interest. Two groups with particularly high prestige are the *Eton Group* (12 schools including, as well as Eton College, Dulwich College, Marlborough College, St Paul's and Westminster) and the *Rugby Group* (17 schools, including, as well as Rugby, Charterhouse, Harrow, Shrewsbury, Stowe and Winchester College). Between them, the schools in the Eton and Rugby Groups have about 20,000 pupils, fewer than 1% of the population in their age group (Walford, 1986, Table 1.1).

- *Society of Headmasters and Headmistresses of Independent Schools (SHMIS)* and *Governing Bodies Association (GBA)* – Most of the 84 schools in the SHMIS also belong to the GBA, which has 306 schools. The GBA schools have 190,000 pupils, 73% of whom are boys, and 23% full or weekly boarders.
- *Girls' Schools Association (GSA)* and *Governing Bodies of Girls' Schools Association (GBGSA)* – The GSA and GBGSA have largely overlapping membership – some 220 schools in all. They are almost exclusively for girls (97% of their 111,000 pupils); 12% are full or weekly boarders.
- *Independent Schools Association (ISA)* – The ISA schools have some 65,000 pupils, with roughly equal numbers of boys and girls; 6% of these are full or weekly boarders.

Overall, about 55% of pupils in these schools are boys, 45% girls (ISIS, 1999).

In Scotland (as in most of the rest of the world), the term 'public schools' usually refers to maintained schools. The term is not used in Northern Ireland, although a few of the voluntary schools (see Chapter 6) belong to the Headmasters' Conference.

Non-maintained schools

This is a term formerly used in the official government statistics for Great Britain, though now largely replaced by the term 'independent schools'. It used to cover voluntary grammar schools in Northern Ireland too, but they are now classified as maintained schools.

Age

	5	8	11	13	16	18
Pupil 1	State primary school		Independent secondary school		Sixth form in local compre-hensive	
Pupil 2	Preparatory school		Independent secondary school for girls		Co-ed sixth form of boys' pub-lic school	
Pupil 3	State first school	Preparatory school (boarding)		Independent public school	State sixth form college	
Pupil 4	State primary school		Independent co-educational secondary school			

Figure 5.14   Some patterns of schooling

Private schools

'Private schools' has a narrow sense, now archaic, in which it refers to schools run for profit by teacher–entrepreneurs (a minority, especially at secondary level); in this sense, the term 'private schools' is *opposed* to 'public schools', which are not profit-making. However, the phrase 'private schools' is nowadays more often applied (as in almost every other country) to independent schools generally; in this sense, it *includes* public schools.

Preparatory schools

These schools take boys from about eight and girls from about 11 until 13 and prepare them for competitive entry to the public schools. Many belong to the Incorporated Association of Preparatory Schools (IAPS), which has approximately 133,000 pupils, of whom 63% are boys. 10% of pupils in IAPS schools are full or weekly boarders (ISIS, 1999).

F A C T   In 1995–6 there were 2,436 independent schools in the United Kingdom, excluding the independent special schools, but including 15 City Technology Colleges. They provided education for some 589,600 children, 6.2% of the total school population (7.0% in England, 4.0% in Scotland, 2.0% in Wales, and 0.3% in Northern Ireland) (GSS, 1997, Tables 13a and 15; GSS, 1998, Table 5.1).

Children may move between the independent and maintained sectors at different stages of their school career; many different patterns of schooling are possible: some of these are illustrated in Figure 5.15.

(F) TERTIARY

The term 'tertiary education' is used for non-compulsory, post-school education, and covers both *further education* and *higher education*. 'Further education' usually refers to courses of A-level standard or below, and 'higher education' to courses above A-level standard or its equivalent; this usage will be followed here.

Both the further and the higher education sectors have undergone substantial change in recent years, as a result of (in England and Wales) the 1988 Education Reform Act and the 1992 Further and Higher Education Act (which has a Scottish counterpart) (see Chapter 4). Further education in Northern Ireland has also been reorganised recently.

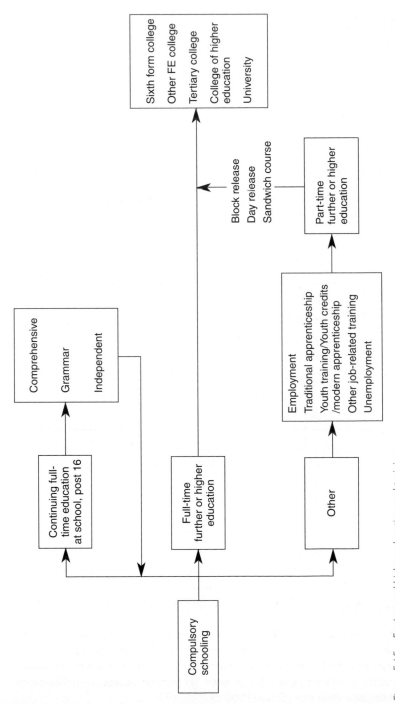

Figure 5.15 Further and higher education and training

FURTHER EDUCATION

Until the 1992 Acts, further education in Britain was financed and controlled by local education authorities (LEAs in England and Wales, EAs in Scotland). Thereafter, further education colleges became corporate bodies independent of local authorities, and financed by the central government. In England and Wales, this funding is indirect, provided on the advice of the Further Education Funding Council (FEFC) and the Further Education Funding Council for Wales. In Scotland, further education is currently under the direct control of the Secretary of State, but a Scottish Further Education Council will assume control in 1999. In Northern Ireland, following the recommendations of a Further Education Review Group, the 24 further education colleges were reduced by mergers to 17. From 1998, they are financed directly by the DENI.

> **F A C T**   In the United Kingdom in 1995–6, there were over 764,000 full-time students (including 'sandwich' students) and 2.8 million part-time students in further education. Over two-thirds of the full-time students (69%) were aged 16–18. They represented about a quarter of the population aged 16–18. Two-thirds of the part-time students were over 25 (ONS, 1998, Tables 2.1 and 5.6).

Sixth form colleges

These were transferred from the schools sector (and LEA control) to the further education sector by the 1992 Further and Higher Education Act. They are separate establishments for 16–19-year-olds, usually taking students from several 'feeder' comprehensive schools without sixth forms in the area, and catering for about 500 students. They may provide non-academic as well as academic courses, but academic courses predominate. In 1973, there were 21 sixth form colleges in England; by 1996 there were 110. Their increase has been partly in response to declining numbers of secondary school pupils, which makes it difficult for many smaller schools to make up viable sixth form classes in less popular A-level subjects.

Tertiary colleges

Tertiary colleges combine the functions of a sixth form college and a further education college. They are open to students of all abilities, and provide a wide range of vocational and academic courses. Some cater for several thousand students, full- and part-time. There were 51 tertiary colleges in England in 1994, and seven in Wales (Evans, M. et al. (ed.), 1994).

Colleges of further education

There are about 550 colleges of further education in the United Kingdom. They go by a variety of titles, including colleges of further education, colleges of agriculture and horticulture, technical colleges, colleges of art and colleges of commerce. They also offer a wide variety of types and levels of courses.

Independent further education colleges

A number of FE colleges outside the publicly maintained system offer full-time and part-time courses in subjects such as art and architecture, drama, languages, and English for foreign students. Their qualifications are validated either by the British Accreditation Council for Independent Further and Higher Education (BACIFHE) or by one of the independent professional bodies such as the National Council for Drama Training or the Council for Dance Education, or are the college's own non-validated certificates or diplomas. Tutorial colleges, sometimes known as 'crammers', are privately run establishments offering intensive courses to prepare students for particular examinations, usually GCSE or A levels.

HIGHER EDUCATION

> **F A C T** There are 176 publicly funded institutions of higher education in the United Kingdom – 137 in England, 21 in Scotland, 14 in Wales, and four in Northern Ireland – with a total of 1.7 million students (HEFCE, 1997, p. v).

From the mid-1960s until the early 1990s, higher education was a 'binary system', with the universities divided from polytechnics (in England, Wales and Northern Ireland), central institutions (in Scotland) and other colleges of higher education. The universities were funded by the central government, but indirectly, through the University Grants Committee, allowing them a substantial degree of autonomy. The polytechnics and other colleges were financed and controlled by local education authorities in England and Wales, and directly by the central government in Scotland. The universities awarded their own degrees; the polytechnics and other colleges had to have their degrees validated by the Council for National Academic Awards (CNAA), or by a university.

The binary division was formally dissolved by the 1992 Further and Higher Education Act and its Scottish counterpart.

- The funding of higher education was unified, with three Higher Education Funding Councils, one each for England, Scotland and Wales. (The English HEFC also advises on the funding of higher education in Northern Ireland.) All higher education establishments in each country now have to compete for the same pool of funds.
- The CNAA was abolished, and most of the institutions whose degrees it had validated acquired the right to award their own degrees. Some smaller colleges of higher education still have to have their degrees externally validated. This is now usually done by a university, in many cases the Open University, which has assumed some of the residual functions of the CNAA.
- If they met certain criteria, polytechnics and other colleges were permitted to take the title of university: all 34 polytechnics, five central institutions and two colleges of higher education have done so, and the number of universities in the United Kingdom has thus almost doubled since 1992.

Since 1992, student numbers in higher education have grown substantially, from about 1,050,000 in 1992–3 to 1,350,000 in 1995–6. However, two qualifications to this picture should be noted. First, about a quarter of the apparent increase in numbers is accounted for by the re-classification of certain existing students – such as student nurses when colleges of nursing merged with other colleges within the higher education sector. Secondly, the percentage of *full-time* students has declined in the same period from about 70% to 65% of all students, as a result of a Government decision in 1994–5 to restrict further growth of full-time students (HEFCE, 1997, p. vi).

Colleges and institutes of higher education

There are 53 colleges and institutes of higher education in the United Kingdom that do not have full university status. In England and Wales, most of these were formed in the 1970s when teacher training was integrated with the rest of higher education outside universities by the merger of colleges of education, technical colleges etc. into larger establishments. As well as teaching qualifications, colleges of higher education generally provide other degree and diploma courses, and so are similar to universities though usually much smaller (with an average of around 2,000 students, compared with 12–14,000 for a typical university). Until 1992, their degrees had to be validated by the CNAA (or a university). After 1992, two colleges of higher education, Derbyshire and Luton, became universities. In addition, 19 of the remaining colleges were empowered to award their own degrees; from 1998, they may call themselves *university colleges*. The remaining 34 colleges must have their degrees validated by a university.

Polytechnics

Polytechnics came into existence after 1966, and ceased to exist as a separate category after 1992, when they became universities. Almost all were in England, which ultimately had 33; Wales and Northern Ireland had one each, though the latter merged in 1985 with the New University of Ulster to form the University of Ulster. (For Scotland, see *Central Institutions*.) Courses at polytechnics were often multi-disciplinary in content and modular in structure, with a technical or vocational emphasis. Polytechnics frequently had close links with business and industry, and their students, unlike those at the older universities, frequently had jobs and studied on a part-time or sandwich basis. Polytechnics also offered some further education courses, but the majority of these were taught at colleges of further education and other colleges of higher education.

Central Institutions

Until 1992, Scotland had 16 Central Institutions, which were similar in function to polytechnics in England and Wales, though they were controlled centrally by the Scottish Education Department rather than by local education authorities, and were more narrowly vocational in their courses than most polytechnics. After 1992, with some re-organization and merger, they formed five new universities, three multi-faculty colleges of higher education, three colleges of education, two colleges of art and the Royal Scottish Academy of Music and Drama. All are now funded through the Scottish Higher Education Funding Council.

Universities

Until the 1992 Further and Higher Education Act and its Scottish counterpart, there were about 50 universities in the United Kingdom (the exact figure depending on whether a number of establishments are counted as colleges of the Universities of London, Wales and Manchester, or as universities in their own right). Now there are about 90, as all the polytechnics, six Central Institutions and two colleges of higher education have been granted university status. They are often classified, very roughly, along lines such as the following (see Bligh, 1990; Burnett et al, 1997).

- *Ancient universities* – There are six of these, all more than 500 years old. Two are English (Oxford and Cambridge) and four Scottish (St Andrew's, Glasgow, Aberdeen and Edinburgh).
- *'Redbrick' or older civic universities* – These were founded in the later 19th century, usually in industrial cities (e.g. Leeds, Manchester).

- *Newer civic universities* – These were created after the Second World War by raising an existing college, often one that had prepared students for external degrees of the University of London, to university status (e.g. Newcastle, Leicester).
- *New universities* – Again, after the Second World War, some entirely new institutions were created (e.g. Kent, Stirling).
- *The former Colleges of Advanced Technology (CATs)* – These were an entire category of institution, given university status after 1964 (e.g. Aston, Strathclyde).
- *The post-1992 universities* – These are: all the former polytechnics, plus six former Central Institutions and two former colleges of higher education (e.g. Huddersfield, Glasgow Caledonian, Luton).

Traditionally, undergraduate courses at university have occupied three or four years of full-time study, but in recent years this has become much more varied and flexible. For example, the first degree courses at the University of Buckingham last only two years, the Open University has part-time students who study by correspondence, and the post-1992 universities have large numbers of part-time and 'sandwich' students.

The Department for Education and Employment has ultimate responsibility for universities in England; those in the other countries of the United Kingdom are the responsibility of the Scottish Office Education and Industry Department, the Welsh Office Education Department and the Department of Education Northern Ireland. But universities have a substantial and jealously guarded degree of independence. They appoint their own staff, decide on their own admissions policies and have traditionally had academic freedom in their teaching and research, though the last of these has arguably been eroded in recent years by the 'earmarking' of government funds for specific subjects, and the need to seek commercial sponsors for particular projects.

With one exception, all universities receive central government funding, which is allocated among them on the basis of advice by the appropriate Higher Education Funding Council (HEFC) rather than by the direct decision of the government. The exception is the University of Buckingham, which receives no government funds.

In 1995–6, universities in England had 1.1 million students – an increase of 30% since 1992–3. About 80% were undergraduates, 20% postgraduates. 'Mature students' (those aged 21 or more when they began their studies for undergraduates, 25 or more for postgraduates) accounted for 45% of all students (HEFCE, 1997, page xiv).

The Open University (OU), established in 1969, teaches by correspondence and broadcasting. It is 'open' in the sense of not requiring any entrance qualifications for its undergraduate courses; admission is on a 'first come first served' basis. It has the largest number of students of any university in the

United Kingdom. In 1997, it had 164,000 registered students – 76% undergraduates, 24% postgraduates. Almost all were mature students, studying part-time. (The average age of undergraduate students was 37.) Over 80% remained in employment during their studies. An additional 50,000 'study packs' were sold during the year to people who did not register as students. The OU accounted for about a fifth of all part-time students in higher education in the United Kingdom (OU Public Relations Department, 1998; HEFCE, 1997, Fig. B).

Apart from the OU, the largest university by far is the University of London which has 90,000 full-time students, followed by the University of Wales with 37,000. However, both are federations of effectively independent colleges (22 for London, 6 for Wales) that are sometimes regarded as universities in their own right. Apart from them, universities range in size from the Manchester Metropolitan University, with 28,000 students, to Cranfield University, with 3,000. The most common university size is between 12,000 and 14,000 students (HEFCE, 1997; HESA, 1996).

About half of all entrants in the 1990s to full-time first-degree courses in universities go on to obtain first class or upper-second class honours degrees. Just under a fifth of all entrants drop out without completing their degree (DfEE/OFSTED, 1998, Tables 2.11 and 2.12).

SOURCES AND FURTHER READING

Bligh, D. (1990) *Higher Education*, London: Cassell.

Burnett, J., Saul, S. B. and Harrison, D. (1997) 'The universities of the United Kingdom', in Association of Commonwealth Universities (1997) *Commonwealth Universities Yearbook 1997–8*, Volume 2, London: Association of Commonwealth Universities.

CSO (1994) *Social Trends*, No. 24, London: HMSO.

CSO (1995) *Social Trends*, No. 25, London: HMSO.

DES (1986) *Statistics of Education: Schools 1986*, London: DES.

DES (1989) *Statistical Bulletin 8/89: Statistics of Schools in England – January 1988*, London: DES.

DFE (1994) *Statistical Bulletin 6/94: Pupils under five years of age in school in England – January 1993*, London: DFE.

DFE (1995) *Statistical Bulletin 2/95: Pupils under five years of age in school in England – January 1995*, London: DFE.

Evans, M. et al (ed.) (1994) *Education Year Book 1995*, Harrow: Longman.

GSS (1983) *Education Statistics for the United Kingdom: 1983 edition*, London: HMSO.

GSS (1985) *Education Statistics for the United Kingdom: 1985 edition*, London: HMSO.

GSS (1989) *Education Statistics for the United Kingdom: 1989 edition*, London: HMSO.

GSS (1994) *Education Statistics for the United Kingdom: 1993 edition*, London: HMSO.

GSS (1997) *Education Statistics for the United Kingdom: 1996 edition*, London: The Stationery Office.

GSS (1998) *Annual Abstract of Statistics: 1998 edition*, London: The Stationery Office.

HEFCE (1997) *Profiles of Higher Education Institutions*, Bristol: Higher Education Funding Council for England.

HESA (1996) *Higher Education Statistics for the United Kingdom 1994/95*, Cheltenham: Higher Education Statistics Agency.

ISIS (1999) *ISIS Annual Census 1999*, London: Independent Schools Information Service.

NISRA (1998) *Northern Ireland Annual Abstract of Statistics*, Belfast: Northern Ireland Statistics and Research Agency.

ONS (1997) *Regional Trends 32*, London: The Stationery Office: HMSO.

ONS (1998) *Monthly Digest of Statistics: June 1998*, London: The Stationery Office: HMSO.

OU Public Relations Department (1998) *Basic Facts and Figures for 1998 (Fact Sheet No. 2)*, Milton Keynes: The Open University.

Walford, G. (1986) *Life in Public Schools*, London: Methuen.

The United Kingdom is on the threshold of profound but unpredictable change, with devolved governments taking office in mid-1999 in Scotland, Wales and (subject to negotiations still in progress as we go to press) Northern Ireland. The Scottish Parliament and the Northern Ireland Assembly will have full powers to enact, repeal and amend legislation within their areas of responsibility, which include education. The Welsh National Assembly will have powers to enact 'secondary legislation' in its areas of responsibility (again including education) to meet distinctive Welsh circumstances (see ONS, 1999, Chapters 3, 4 and 5).

In this edition, however, we describe the organisation and control of education in these countries as it stands in early 1999, as we go to press.

Even before devolution, the four countries of the UK have separate education systems. In England, education and vocational training are the responsibility of the Department for Education and Employment. In the other countries, responsibility for education and training currently lies with the Scottish, Welsh and Northern Ireland Offices of the UK Government, but it will be transferred to the new parliament or assembly in each country.

Though separate, the education systems in England and in Wales are currently very similar, educational legislation often applies to both countries, and policy documents and directives are often issued jointly in the names of the Secretary of State for Education and Employment and the Secretary of State for Wales. Scotland and Northern Ireland differ in a number of significant ways from England and Wales, and from one another. Most importantly, Scotland has different curriculum and examination arrangements from the other three countries, which are more similar to one another. And Northern Ireland retains a system of selective secondary schooling, whereas maintained secondary schools in the other three countries are almost all comprehensive.

In all four countries of the UK, education is administered as a partnership between central government and local education authorities, though the balance of power and influence between the partners is changing, with local authorities steadily losing powers. At local level, the education authorities in England, Wales and Scotland are the elected local councils, which have many other responsibilities besides education, but in Northern Ireland they are centrally appointed bodies ('Education and Library Boards') separate from the elected local councils.

ENGLAND AND WALES

Central government

The central government department responsible for education and training in England is the Department for Education and Employment (DfEE). Its formal educational responsibilities cover all schools (maintained and independent), further education (FE), higher education (HE), and youth and adult pre-vocational and vocational training. In practice, however, much of the administration of these areas is delegated to a variety of national and local bodies. The DfEE is also responsible for some aspects of the teaching profession in Wales.

The Office for Standards in Education is a non-ministerial department independent of the DfEE (see below).

Like all government departments, the DfEE has a dual structure of ministers, who are elected politicians, and civil servants who remain in post irrespective of changes of government. The DfEE has as its political head a cabinet minister,

Minister of State (Estelle Morris)	Minister of State (Tessa Blackstone)	Minister of State (Andrew Smith)
School standards	Lifelong learning	Employment
Teachers	Training, skills and employability	Labour market statistics
School organisation		EU and international (employment)
School funding	Public service reform	
School-industry links	EU and international (education)	Regional and urban policy
		Competitiveness
		Equal opportunities

Parliamentary Undersecretary of State (Charles Clarke)	Parliamentary Undersecretary of State (Kim Howells)	Parliamentary Undersecretary of State (Alan Howarth)
School standards	Lifelong learning	Employment
Teachers	Training, skills and employability	Child care
School organisation	IT and new technologies	Work permits
Early years education	Constitutional reform	Millenium volunteers
Pupil issues	Public/private partnerships	Equal opportunities
Special educational needs	Teachers	
'Section 11'	Green issues	

Figure 6.1   Responsibilities of DfEE junior ministers
(Adapted from DfEE/OFSTED, 1998, page 16)

the Secretary of State for Education and Employment – currently David Blunkett, as we go to press. He is assisted at present by six junior ministers, three Ministers of State (the more senior level) and three Parliamentary Undersecretaries of State. Their main responsibilities are shown (under the names of the ministers in office as we go to press) in Figure 6.1 Where two or more ministers have responsibilities for a particular area, there is normally a division of labour between them. For example, three ministers have responsibilities for teachers: of these, Ms Morris is responsible for teachers' pay and conditions; Mr Clarke for their training, misconduct, qualifications, supply and appraisal; and Dr Howells for their pensions. (For more detail, see DfEE/OFSTED, 1998, p. 16, though it lists the names of the predecessors of some of these ministers.)

The civil service side of the DfEE consists at national level of an executive agency, the Employment Service, plus seven directorates. Three of these directorates are directly concerned with education: their main responsibilities are shown in Figure 6.2. (The other directorates are concerned respectively with: Finance and analytical services; Personnel and support services; Strategy and communications; and Operations.) As Figures 6.1 and 6.2 show, the divisions of responsibility among ministers and among directorates do not match exactly.

In 1997–8, the DfEE employed just under 36,000 staff (86% of them in the Employment Service). This represents a reduction in staff numbers of 38% since 1992–3. A further 500 full-time staff are employed by OFSTED.

In addition, there are ten regional government offices, which have regional responsibilities for implementing the programmes of the DfEE (such as the

Schools	Further Education, Higher Education and Youth Training	Employment and Lifelong Learning
Organisation and buildings	Higher Education and student support	Employment policy
Curriculum, funding and teachers	Qualifications and occupational standards	Equal opportunities, technologies and overseas labour
Pupils, parents and youth	Further Education	Skills and lifelong learning
Standards and effectiveness	Education and training policy for 16–19 year olds	International
Communications		'New Deal' project
Education Bill		

Figure 6.2   *Responsibilities of the DfEE directorates most directly concerned with education (Adapted from DfEE/OFSTED, 1998, p. 17)*

management of contracts with TECs – see Chapter 12 below) as well as those of other governmental departments. (The regions are listed in Chapter 2.)

In Wales, education is the responsibility of the Education Department and training of the Industry and Training Department of the Welsh Office. The Office of Her Majesty's Chief Inspector of Schools in Wales is independent of the Education Department. In 1997–8, the Education Department employed 82 staff, the Industry and Training Department 155, and the Office of Her Majesty's Chief Inspector of Schools 59.

Local government

Local government in England is complicated. In some parts of the country there are unitary authorities, each performing all the functions of local government in the area it covers. In other parts, there are tiers of authorities with local government responsibilities divided between them. In total, 150 of these local authorities function as local education authorities (LEAs). These consist of 46 unitary authorities, 36 metropolitan districts, 34 counties, 20 outer London boroughs, 12 inner London boroughs plus the City of London, and the Scilly Isles. (See Figures 6.3, 6.4 and 6.5.)

In Wales, there are 22 LEAs – all corresponding to unitary local authorities. (See Figure 6.3.)

The LEAs in England and Wales are part of local authorities with wider responsibilities. Mirroring the central government division between ministers and civil servants, they are divided between elected councillors and appointed education officers. They function through education committees, on which elected councillors form a majority. In most LEAs, the education committee has several subcommittees: usually one for finance and at least one for schools (larger authorities may have separate ones for primary, secondary and special schools), at least one for further education and possibly others for careers, libraries and museums, and sites and buildings.

Traditionally, the control of state education in England and Wales has been shared between central and local government, the former responsible for general policy, the latter for its detailed implementation. But in the 1980s and 1990s, many responsibilities for education have been or are now being taken from the LEAs and transferred, on the one hand to central government and government-appointed bodies (the so-called quangos – 'quasi-autonomous non-governmental organisations'); and on the other hand to the governing bodies (see below) of individual schools and colleges.

Now most of the school curriculum and its assessment is determined by government ministers, with advice from the Qualifications and Curriculum Authority (for England) and the Qualifications, Curriculum and Assessment Authority for Wales, bodies whose members are appointed by government ministers. Religious education is still determined locally. (See Chapter 10.)

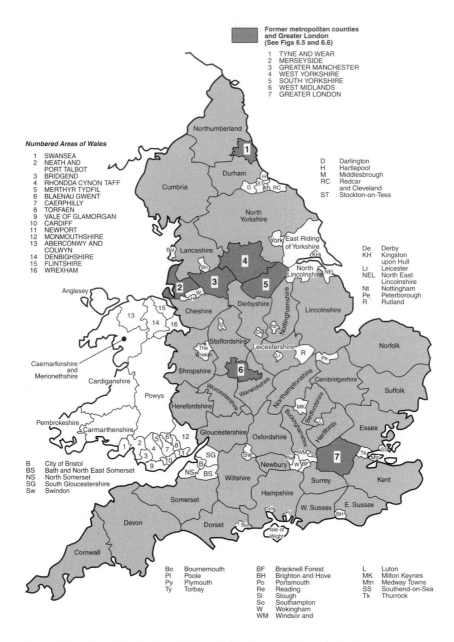

Former metropolitan counties
and Greater London
(See Figs 6.5 and 6.6)

1   TYNE AND WEAR
2   MERSEYSIDE
3   GREATER MANCHESTER
4   WEST YORKSHIRE
5   SOUTH YORKSHIRE
6   WEST MIDLANDS
7   GREATER LONDON

Numbered Areas of Wales

1   SWANSEA
2   NEATH AND
    PORT TALBOT
3   BRIDGEND
4   RHONDDA CYNON TAFF
5   MERTHYR TYDFIL
6   BLAENAU GWENT
7   CAERPHILLY
8   TORFAEN
9   VALE OF GLAMORGAN
10 CARDIFF
11 NEWPORT
12 MONMOUTHSHIRE
13 ABERCONWY AND
    COLWYN
14 DENBIGHSHIRE
15 FLINTSHIRE
16 WREXHAM

D   Darlington
H   Hartlepool
M   Middlesbrough
RC   Redcar
     and Cleveland
ST   Stockton-on-Tees

De   Derby
KH   Kingston
     upon Hull
Lr   Leicester
NEL North East
     Lincolnshire
Nt   Nottingham
Pe   Peterborough
R   Rutland

B   City of Bristol
BS   Bath and North East Somerset
NS   North Somerset
SG   South Gloucestershire
Sw   Swindon

Bo   Bournemouth
Pl   Poole
Py   Plymouth
Ty   Torbay

BF   Bracknell Forest
BH   Brighton and Hove
Po   Portsmouth
Re   Reading
Sl   Slough
So   Southampton
W   Wokingham
WM   Windsor and

L   Luton
MK   Milton Keynes
Mtn Medway Towns
SS   Southend-on-Sea
Tk   Thurrock

Figure 6.3   LEAs of England and Wales: (i) Counties and Unitary Authorities

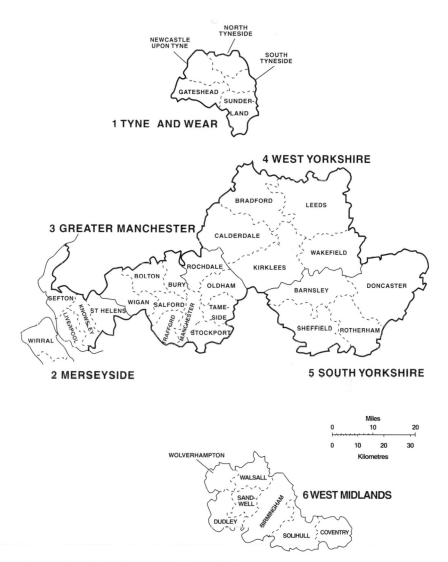

Figure 6.4   LEAs of England and Wales: (ii) Metropolitan districts of England

Schools in the state sector ('maintained schools') are mostly still financed by LEAs, but this no longer gives the LEAs much control or influence over them. Under the system known as local management of schools (LMS), the total amount of money to be given to each school under a LEA must now be determined by a standard formula, approved by the central government. It must

Figure 6.5   LEAs of England and Wales: (iii) London boroughs (and the City)

INNER LONDON
 1   CITY OF LONDON
 2   ISLINGTON
 3   CAMDEN
 4   WESTMINSTER
 5   KENSINGTON AND CHELSEA
 6   HAMMERSMITH AND FULHAM
 7   WANDSWORTH
 8   LAMBETH
 9   SOUTHWARK
10   LEWISHAM
11   GREENWICH
12   TOWER HAMLETS
13   HACKNEY

place most weight on the numbers of pupils in the school, and must be applied even-handedly across all the authority's schools. (Finance cannot now be used by LEAs as a means of influencing the policy or practice of a school.) The allocation of this money among textbooks and equipment, building repairs, teachers' salaries and so on is now decided by the governing body of each individual school, as is the appointment and dismissal of individual teachers.

Besides, a relatively small but highly visible number of maintained schools in England and Wales have become grant-maintained schools – just over 1,100 in

1995–6, nearly 4% of all primary and secondary schools. They have left the control of LEAs entirely, and receive their funding from the central government, not LEAs. In England, the funds are currently distributed by a quango, the Funding Agency for Schools (FAS), whose members are chosen by the Secretary of State for Education and Employment. In addition to their responsibilities for funding grant-maintained schools, the FAS has been able to assume some or all of the responsibilities currently held by LEAs for the planning of educational provision in their areas, if the percentage of pupils in a LEA's area who attend grant-maintained primary or secondary schools reached a specified percentage. However, with the 1998 School Standards and Framework Act, the category of grant-maintained schools is to be replaced in 2000 by that of foundation schools, and the FAS is to be dissolved. (See Chapter 4 and p. 112 below.) Wales's 16 grant-maintained schools are financed directly by the Welsh Office.

From September 1998, the role of LEAs in England is further modified as the first Education Action Zones come into operation. Education Action Zones are being established in 'areas with a mix of underperforming schools and the highest levels of social disadvantage' (DfEE/OFSTED, 1998, p. 27). They receive extra funding (currently about £1 million extra per zone per year), and are given freedom to experiment, for example with the curriculum, the pay and conditions of teachers, the length of the school day, and the involvement of business people in management.

For an Education Action Zone to be formed, a local partnership must form and bid to the Secretary of State for Action Zone status. These partnerships may involve any combination of interested parties, incuding LEAs, schools, parents and business people. A successful partnership will form an Action Forum, which will run the Zone, setting and monitoring an Action Plan for the Zone as a whole and for each school within it. The governing bodies of these schools may pass on all or some of their powers to the Action Forum, or retain these powers and work in collaboration with it.

The first 25 Education Action Zones were named by the Secretary of State in June 1998, chosen from 60 applicants. The Zones each have about 20 schools, consisting of a cluster of secondary schools with supporting primary schools and associated provision for children with special educational needs. In almost all of the first batch of successful applications, the LEA took the leading role in the partnership. In one case (Lambeth), however, a central role was played by Shell International, and the Zone will be run by an equal partnership of the LEA and a private, though non-profit-making, education management company. There is a further round of bidding in early 1999 (DfEE/OFSTED, 1998; Carvel, 1998).

In tertiary education, the universities have always been independent of local authorities, but until the 1980s and 1990s, the polytechnics and other institutions of higher and further education in England and Wales were run by the

LEAs. Now, though, the polytechnics have become universities (see Chapter 5), and the universities, colleges of higher education and most further education colleges are autonomous bodies funded by the government through quangos – the Higher Education Funding Council and the Further Education Funding Council for each country.

The current distribution of powers and duties between central government, LEAs, headteachers, school governors and parents in England and Wales is summarised in Figure 6.6.

County and voluntary schools

The 1944 Education Act created a unified framework which brought the church schools under state control (turning them into maintained schools), but left them with varying degrees of independence, according to how much financial support the church continued to provide. This system has remained unchanged until the 1998 School Standards and Framework Act, which replaces it (from 2000) with a new framework – albeit a fairly similar one (see below).

The LEAs created by the 1944 Act could set up new schools themselves; these are called *county schools*. Schools that had been established by a church body (or occasionally a trust) became *voluntary schools*, of which there are three types: 'aided', 'controlled' and 'special agreement', differing mainly in the extent to which the LEA finances and controls them.

- *Aided schools* (about 4,300 in number in England in the early 1990s, roughly half Church of England and half Roman Catholic) provide their own premises and meet some of the maintenance costs in exchange for a degree of control.
- *Controlled schools* (3,000 in number in England, virtually all Church of England) provide their own premises, but the LEAs meet all the schools' costs. Before the 1988 Act, the governing bodies had control only over religious instruction.
- *Special agreement schools* are few in number (77, most of them Roman Catholic), and they arose from the government's offer in 1936 to pay 50–75% of the cost of building new secondary schools.

And, as mentioned above, the 1988 Education Reform Act established a further category, *grant-maintained schools*.

- *Grant-maintained schools* (just over 1,100 in England and Wales in 1995–6) are mostly maintained schools whose governing bodies and parents have chosen to 'opt out' of LEA finance and control – though the 1993 Education Act has introduced further ways of establishing them. They own their premises and employ their staff, receiving grants from central government via the Funding Agency for Schools (in England) or the Welsh Office.

DfEE/WOED	LEA	Headteacher	Parents	Governors
Policy making	Provide 'adequate and efficient' education at primary and secondary level (nursery optional)	Care of pupils ('in loco parentis')	Send child to school (or 'educate otherwise')	Oversee implementation of national curriculum, conduct and discipline
Inspecting all schools and institutions		Internal organisation of school	Express preference for a school	Financial management of school
Supply and training of teachers	Establish, alter and close schools (after giving public notice)	Rules, discipline, curriculum (subject to national curriculum and governors' general direction)	Be represented on governing body	Appointment and dismissal of teachers
Final court of appeal in disputes between parents and LEA	Finance non-GM schools and local education service	Financial management of school (in association with governors)	Receive published information about school	Suspension/expulsion of pupils
Providing education support grants	Enforce school attendance		Be involved in assessment procedure for children with special educational needs	Sex education
Financing further education (via FEFCs)	Identify and provide for special educational needs		Withdraw child from religious or sex education	Use 'best endeavours' to identify children with special educational needs
Financing higher education (via HEFCs)	Health and safety		Decide whether a school should 'opt out' of LEA control	Publish information for parents about the school
Collecting statistics	Careers service			
Educational building programme	Ensure equal opportunities for both sexes and all races			

Figure 6.6   Powers and duties

Services that cannot practicably be provided by a single school may be purchased from LEAs, or provided by a consortium of two or more grant-maintained schools. Grant-maintained schools remain subject to the national curriculum and its associated tests, and to inspection by OFSTED. They may not change their character (e.g. from comprehensive to selective) without permission from the Secretary of State, though in a number of cases such permission has been sought and given. Since the 1993 Act, independent schools may 'opt in' to grant-maintained status, or entirely new schools may be set up within the grant-maintained sector, on the initiative of local 'promoters' or of the Funding Agency.

The main differences in funding and control between the different traditional types of school are summarised in Figure 6.7.

Voluntary schools in England account for about a third of primary schools and a fifth of secondary schools (see Figure 6.8). The majority of voluntary primary schools are Church of England, while just over half of voluntary secondary schools are Roman Catholic. Voluntary schools in Wales account for about 15% of all schools (primary and secondary) – 10% Church in Wales (Anglican) and 5% Roman Catholic.

As noted above, this 1944/1988 framework is to be replaced in 2000. The new framework has five main categories of school:

- community
- foundation
- voluntary (aided or controlled)
- community special
- foundation special

Community, foundation and voluntary schools will correspond roughly to the existing county, grant-maintained and voluntary schools. Governing bodies may choose to have their school join the category corresponding to its present status, or to ballot parents to seek approval to join another category. All the new categories of school will receive their recurrent funding from LEAs, and will continue to manage their own delegated budgets. A clear distinction is to be drawn between functions that must be financed and provided centrally by the LEAs, and functions that will be the responsibility of the schools. All schools will continue to be run by governing bodies, with members representing the local community, the LEA, school staff, parents and (for church schools) churches, but the number of parent governors will be increased.

SCOTLAND

The central government department responsible for education in Scotland is the *Scottish Office Education and Industry Department* (SOEID). It is responsible

	Maintained schools				Independent schools
	County	Voluntary			
		Aided	Controlled	Special agreement	
Established by:	LEA	Voluntary organisations, usually religious bodies – C of E, Church in Wales, Roman Catholic Church, Jewish organisations		Voluntary organisations usually church bodies – but by special agreement the LEA pays 50–75% cost of building a new school	Private individuals Benefactors Trust and charities
Financed by:	LEA	Voluntary body responsible for external repairs and maintenance (assisted by 85% LEA grant) LEA pays running costs, internal repairs and teachers' salaries	LEA	Voluntary body responsible for external repairs and maintenance (assisted by 85% LEA grant)	Parental fees Assisted places scheme Benefactors/charities
Controlled by:	LEA and governing body Must offer non-denominational religious instruction to all pupils	Voluntary body appoints $\frac{2}{3}$ majority of governors, and hence controls admissions and appointment of teachers Can offer denominational instruction to all pupils	LEA appoints majority of governors, but voluntary body nominates a third Can offer denominational instruction to families who request it	Voluntary body appoints majority of governors	Board of Governors (DfEE can enforce minimum standards for premises and staffing)

Figure 6.7   *The administration and control of traditional schools (i.e. other than grant-maintained schools) in England and Wales*

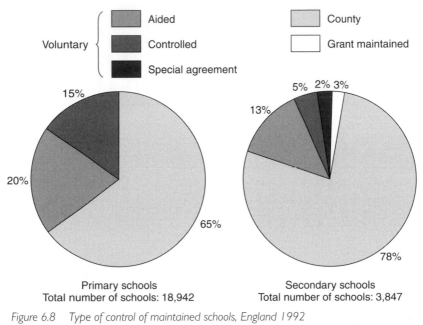

Figure 6.8   Type of control of maintained schools, England 1992
(Adapted from DFE, 1993, Table A13)

for all education in Scotland. Higher education is funded through the Scottish Higher Education Funding Council (SHEFC); further education is at present financed directly by the SOEID, but a Scottish Further Education Funding Council is being established in 1999. As in England and Wales, Scottish local government has recently been radically reorganised. From 1996, there are 32 education authorities (EAs), replacing the previous 12. All are unitary authorities. (See Figure 6.9.)

Scotland has no statutory school curriculum, unlike the other countries of the United Kingdom. Central influence on what schools teach is more indirect (see Chapter 10).

The control of schools

More than three-quarters of Scottish schools have *school boards*, with elected representatives of parents and teachers in addition to co-opted members. However, these do not have the managerial functions of English governing bodies. Their role is advisory and consultative; they provide a channel of communication between school and community; and they play a part in the appointment of senior staff.

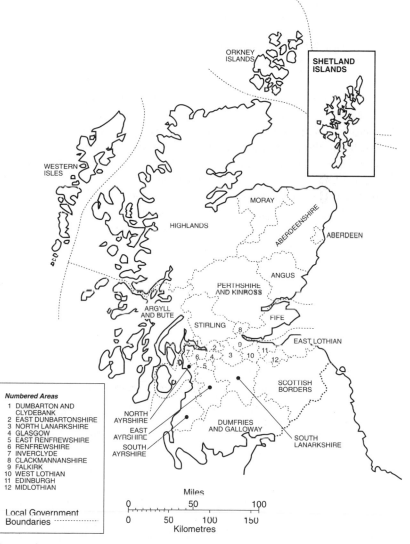

Figure 6.9   Education authorities in Scotland

Scotland does not have voluntary schools. Church schools (mostly Roman Catholic) which chose to transfer to the education authority, rather than be independent, became public schools (the term used in Scotland for maintained or state schools), although they can make separate arrangements for denominational instruction.

The Scottish counterpart to the grant-maintained school is the *self-governing school*. By 1998, there were just two.

NORTHERN IRELAND

The central government department responsible for education in Northern Ireland, the *Department of Education Northern Ireland* (DENI), has overall responsibility for schools, further education and universities. Local education authorities in Northern Ireland are called *Education and Library Boards*, and are responsible for the local provision and administration of schools and further education. There are five of these; their current boundaries date from 1973 (see Figure 6.10). Unlike the local education authorities in Great Britain, Education and Library Boards in Northern Ireland are appointed centrally, by the DENI, though their membership includes nominated representatives of district councils, as well as teachers, local community representatives, trade union nominees, churches and maintained school trustees (see below).

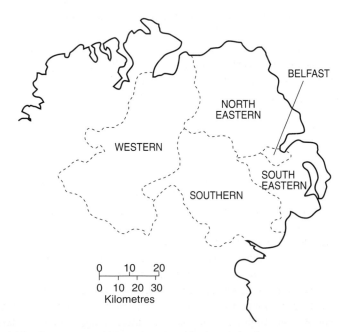

Figure 6.10   Education and Library Boards in Northern Ireland

The control of schools

All publicly financed schools have boards of governors, with elected representatives of parents and teachers. In almost all schools, they manage delegated budgets, and decide on their spending priorities, and on the appointment and deployment of teachers.

Northern Ireland uses the terms 'controlled', 'voluntary' and 'maintained', but with meanings different from those that apply in England and Wales. There are three principal types of school management, described below; in all of them, the representation of parents and teachers has been strengthened, and that of the churches reduced, since 1984.

- *Controlled schools* are managed by Education and Library Boards through boards of governors. The schools may be primary, secondary intermediate, grammar or special; membership of boards of governors differs for the different types of school, but they include representatives of parents, teachers, education and library boards, and sometimes churches (mainly the Protestant churches). The capital expenditure and running costs of controlled schools are met by the Education and Library Boards from funds provided by the DENI. A *controlled integrated school* is a type of school introduced by the 1978 Education (Northern Ireland) Act. The aim was to facilitate the development of schools which would be attended by pupils of different faiths. The proposal to change to a controlled integrated school has to be supported by three-quarters of the parents. Four such schools now exist.
- *Voluntary (maintained) schools* are managed by boards of governors, which consist of representatives of trustees (mainly Roman Catholic), parents, teachers and Education and Library Boards. Capital expenditure on these schools is partly met (up to 85%) by the DENI; running costs are met by the Education and Library Boards. There are several integrated primary voluntary (maintained) schools, and one integrated post-primary (Lagan College).
- *Voluntary (non-maintained) schools* are managed by boards of governors, whose constitutions vary from school to school, but which include representatives of parents and teachers, and sometimes of the DENI or an Education and Library Board. They are mainly grammar schools; there are separate Protestant and Roman Catholic schools. Capital expenditure on these schools is partly met (up to 85%) by the DENI; running costs are met from block grants direct from the DENI and from fees (although for many pupils these are paid or assisted by the Education and Library Boards).
- *Grant-maintained schools* are financed directly by the DENI rather than Education and Library Boards, and must be integrated. By mid-1994 there were 19 such schools.

SOURCES AND FURTHER READING

DFE (1993) *Statistics of Schools 1992*, London: DFE.

DfEE and OFSTED (1998) *Department Report/The Government's Expenditure Plans 1998–99*, Cm 3910, London: The Stationery Office.

Department of Finance and Personnel (Northern Ireland Office)/HM Treasury (1998) *Northern Ireland Expenditure Plans and Priorities: The Government's Expenditure Plans 1998–99*, Cm 3916, London: The Stationery Office.

Departments of the Secretary of State for Scotland/Forestry Commission (1998) *Serving Scotland's Needs: the Government's Expenditure Plans 1998–99*, Cm 3914, Edinburgh: The Stationery Office.

ONS (1999) *Britain: the official yearbook of the United Kingdom*, London: The Stationery Office.

Welsh Office and the Office of Her Majesty's Chief Inspector of Schools in Wales (1998) *The Government's Expenditure Plans 1998–99*, Cm 3915, London: The Stationery Office.

(A) INTRODUCTION

The education service employs a wide variety of staff. Apart from those whose job is to teach (in schools, colleges and universities), there are the administrators, advisers and inspectors; the support staff who assist teachers (e.g. nursery assistants and laboratory assistants); the ancillary workers who maintain premises, provide the meals service and run the offices; and the professionals who offer specialist services, such as the educational psychologists.

> **F A C T**   Out of a total workforce of 1.8 million (excluding police and other law and order services) in 1990, local authorities in England and Wales employed 906,000 (50%) in the education service; 517,000 of these (28% of all employees) were teachers and lecturers. These figures represent a reduction in staffing levels since 1980 of 5% for all employees, 9% for those in education (CIPFA, 1991, Table 5.4).

Figure 7.1 groups jobs in education into five main categories, although in practice the boundaries (e.g. between administrators and advisers) are not always well defined, and the term 'ancillary staff' is sometimes used to cover jobs categorised as 'educational support' too. Most of the staff in Figure 7.1 are employed by the LEA, apart from those in further and higher education and the HMIs, who are employed by the central government. However, the 1988 Local Government Act requires that a local authority's cleaning and maintenance work be put out to competitive tender: this has resulted in fewer of these staff being employed directly by the LEA. And after the 1988 Education Reform Act, teachers, though still formally employed by LEAs, are appointed, and may be dismissed, by the governors of their schools.

(B) THE STAFF OF THE EDUCATION SERVICE

This section gives a brief description of the principal posts in the education service, at the level of central government, LEAs and schools. This is followed by some more detailed facts and figures about the teaching profession, and a description of some of the professionals involved in further and higher education.

LEA administrators	Teaching staff (schools)	Education support staff	Other education professionals	Ancillary staff	Further and higher education
Director of Education/ Chief Education Officer (CEO)	Headteacher	Welfare assistant	Educational psychologist (EP)	Administration and clerical	Vice chancellor/ Principal/Director/ Chief Executive
	Deputy head	Nursery assistant	Education welfare officer (EWO)	Kitchen and canteen	Professor
Deputy CEO	Teacher	Teacher's aide	Adviser	Caretakers	Reader
	Nursery teacher	Specialist teacher assistant	Youth and community worker	Porters	Principal lecturer
Assistant Education Officer (AEO)	Special school teacher	Laboratory technician	Careers officer	Gardeners	Senior lecturer
Professional assistant	Peripatetic teacher	Media resources officer	Schools-industry liaison officer	Cleaners	Lecturer
	Supply teacher	Librarian	Her Majesty's Inspector (HMI)	Security staff	Research fellow
	Home liaison teacher	Medical staff			Research officer
	Home tutor				Research associate
	Educational home visitor				Research assistant

Figure 7.1   Jobs in the education service
(Adapted from CIPFA, no single date)

Central government level

Inspectors

Inspection of schools in England is the responsibility of the Office for Standards in Education (OFSTED), a non-ministerial department (independent of the DFEE) headed by Her Majesty's Chief Inspector of Schools. Before the 1992 Education (Schools) Act (and subsequent regulations issued by the Secretary of State), school inspections had been conducted directly by Her Majesty's Inspectors of Schools (HMIs), full-time professionals attached to, but independent of, the Department of Education and Science. Their principal role was to report to the Secretary of State on the education offered in schools and colleges; they also gave him or her professional advice, were involved in the in-service training of teachers, and helped to disseminate the government's thinking on curriculum and teaching. But now, the full-time professional inspectors are fewer (around 200 instead of just under 500) and play a more administrative and organisational part. OFSTED keeps a register of *Registered Inspectors*, not in the employ of OFSTED but 'fit and proper person[s] ... able to conduct inspections competently and efficiently' (DFE, 1993, p. 4). Actual inspections of schools and colleges are now normally conducted by teams of independent *Inspectors* (not in the employ of OFSTED), headed by a Registered Inspector, and including at least one *Lay Inspector* who has not been involved professionally in education. All the members of the inspection team must normally have successfully completed a course of training organised or approved by OFSTED. A team is offered a contract by OFSTED for the inspection of a school or college, after it has invited tenders from at least two Registered Inspectors. All maintained schools (including grant-maintained schools and CTCs) and some independent schools (notably those catering for children with special educational needs) are to have a six-yearly inspection (more frequent where serious problems are identified), lasting not more than two weeks, and normally not more than one. The inspectors must report on the quality of education provided, the educational standards achieved, the efficiency of financial management and the 'spiritual, moral, social and cultural development' of the pupils (DFE, 1993, p. 5).

OFSTED now also inspects the working of LEAs, and the providers of initial teacher training.

Since mid-1998, there is a new procedure for hearing complaints about OFSTED inspections, headed by the OFSTED Complaints Adjudicator. The Adjudicator, however, is appointed by OFSTED (on a renewable one-year contract) and accountable to OFSTED – a position the first incumbent of the post (Ms E. Rassaby) has described as unsatisfactory (House of Commons, 1998, p. 2, col. 1).

Similar arrangements now obtain in Wales, through the Office of Her Majesty's Chief Inspector of Schools in Wales (OHMCI), which is independent of the Welsh Office Education Department (see Welsh Office/Office of Her Majesty's Chief Inspector of Schools in Wales, 1998, Chapter 9).

In Scotland, however, Her Majesty's Inspectorate retains its traditional twin roles of directly inspecting schools and colleges (and now also publishing reports on individual institutions), and of giving professional advice to ministers and government departments and agencies on the formation of national policy.

Local education authority level

Chief education officer (CEO)
Every LEA is required to have a chief education officer (known in some authorities as the director of education), who is the senior appointed official, with overall administrative responsibility for the running of the local education system. He or she is accountable to the education committee, on which elected councillors form the majority (see Chapter 6).

Deputy chief education officer
He or she coordinates the assistant education officers (see below), and deals with major initiatives such as secondary school reorganisation.

Assistant education officer
An assistant education officer is in charge of one of the half dozen or so branches into which the work of the education service is divided, such as secondary education or further education.

Professional assistant
This is a first-level administrative post within an education department, usually for an experienced teacher. He or she works under an assistant education officer. The post is sometimes also known as administrative assistant.

Adviser (sometimes called inspector)
Advisers are employed by the LEA to advise on the content and quality of courses, organise in-service training of teachers and, in some authorities, to inspect schools and colleges. They are usually responsible for a particular field, such as computing, preschool provision, adult education, political education or equal opportunities. There is no uniformity of numbers; some large authorities have 50 or more advisers while some LEAs have none, relying on OFSTED teams for inspection and advice.

Educational psychologist
Every LEA has a team of educational psychologists headed by a principal educational psychologist. They generally have a psychology degree, a teaching qualification, some teaching experience and further specialist training. They work with children who have behavioural and/or learning problems in school, administering tests (traditional IQ testing used to be a central part of the job,

but it is becoming less important) and designing remedial work in conjunction with teachers. Some educational psychologists visit the schools in their area on a regular basis so that teachers know when they will be coming in and can discuss children they may be worried about; others visit at the request of schools or when a child is formally referred to them. They are part of the LEA's Schools Psychological Service or Child Guidance Service, and are often based in a Child Guidance Clinic. A large proportion of their time is taken up with identifying and assessing children's special educational needs, especially under the procedures introduced by the 1981 Education Act (see Chapter 3). Educational psychologists also work with children under school age who are likely to have special educational needs when they do start school, usually those children with a severe, or early-diagnosed, difficulty.

Education welfare officer (EWO) (also known as education social worker)

Education welfare officers liaise with Social Services Departments and are responsible for the general well-being of school children, not only ensuring that they attend school regularly but also dealing with grants, allowances and services which they may need to be able to attend (e.g. clothing, transport, free school meals). The job involves a substantial amount of fieldwork, such as visiting families where there is a record of absence, lateness or other difficulties at school, and the Educational Welfare Service (staffed by the EWOs) is usually based in the community rather than the Town Hall, in a school or small area office. EWOs are also involved with the families of children who have special educational needs, and in some LEAs they deliver to parents the 'Section 5 Letter' which initiates the formal assessment procedure for such children (see Chapter 13).

Careers officer

LEAs are obliged to set up a Careers Service, which is staffed by careers officers. As with education welfare officers, their job involves travelling in the community rather than being part of the central LEA administration, and so they also generally work in area teams based in a local school. Their job is part counselling, part provider of information. They liaise with secondary school careers teachers, and also with the employers in an area.

Youth and community worker/officer

Although youth work has many of the functions of social work, it is primarily an education service. Most full-time, qualified youth and community workers are employed by LEAs, although a few work for Social Services or Leisure Departments. By far the greater part of youth work, however, is still done by volunteers. Qualified youth and community workers generally have a teaching qualification; some institutions offer a BEd degree or postgraduate courses in youth and community studies. They are generally based in youth clubs and centres, and work on a variety of projects including those for the unemployed.

Schools–industry liaison officer (SILO)

They are appointed by LEAs to coordinate the work of schools and industry within their areas.

School level

Headteacher

Virtually every school in the country has a headteacher who is responsible for the overall running of the school and for the rules, discipline and curriculum, under the direction of the school's governors and subject to any requirements of the LEA and, since the 1988 Education Reform Act, to the national curriculum. While reducing headteachers' autonomy in curricular matters, the 1988 Act increases their responsibility in matters of financial management. Headteachers' salaries are linked to the number of pupils in their schools.

A National Professional Qualification for Headteachers (NPQH) has been introduced by the Teacher Training Agency, and all new heads in England and Wales will be required to hold it. Work is proceeding on comparable qualifications in Scotland (the Scottish Qualification for Headship – SQH) and Northern Ireland.

Deputy headteacher

The deputy head assists the head in the running of a school, often liaising between the head and the rest of the staff. Large secondary schools may have two or more deputy heads, with defined areas of responsibility (e.g. for the curriculum); primary schools normally have one. As with heads, their salaries are linked to the number of pupils in their schools.

Class teacher

Class teachers are the main category of professionals involved in the education of children, and more detailed information about them is given in the next section. Usually one teacher at a time works with a class of children, teaching a particular subject in the case of secondary schools, or teaching virtually all of the curriculum in the case of primary schools. Thus, children in a primary school will spend most of their time with the same teacher in any one year. A less common pattern is for teachers to combine classes and teach together ('team teaching'), usually for particular subjects or in open-plan primary schools.

Special school teacher

Teachers in special schools are paid an additional allowance, but the small size of the schools and the move towards integrating children with special needs into ordinary schools mean that they have fewer prospects for promotion than teachers in mainstream schools. They must be qualified teachers, and in Scotland must have previously taught in an ordinary school for at least a year (this is common practice but not compulsory in England and Wales). Teachers of the deaf, partially hearing and blind must in addition have a specialist qualification, and many other teachers in special schools (and increasingly in ordinary schools too) attend in-service training courses on children with special educational needs. With increasing integration, some special school teachers are spending part of their time in ordinary schools, supporting children with special educational needs in ordinary classes or special classes and units attached to the ordinary school.

Nursery school teacher
A nursery school teacher is a qualified teacher who usually specialises, during training, in the education of nursery and infant children. Nursery school teachers teach in either nursery schools or special nursery classes attached to a primary school, and are helped by nursery assistants and nursery students (doing the practical part of their training).

Nursery assistant
A nursery assistant is not qualified as a teacher, but holds a National Nursery Examination Board (NNEB) qualification (a theoretical and practical course studying the development and care of young children).

Specialist teacher assistant
These play an increasingly important part in primary schools, under a variety of titles (including teaching assistant, classroom assistant and teacher's aide). There are no formal qualifications or training requirements for employment, though an increasing number of assistants are trained, and training courses may be inspected by OFSTED. Teaching assistants work alongside and under the direction of classroom teachers. There are currently some 50,000 (FTE) – about one for every four primary teachers.

Welfare assistant
This is a person without teaching qualifications who is employed by the LEA to work alongside a class teacher, often with a particular child who has special educational needs. His or her job is to deal with the child's physical needs (e.g. arising from incontinence, lack of mobility or impaired speech) rather than to help teach the whole class.

Supply teacher
Each LEA has a supply of teachers who are sent in to schools to cover for absences of regular teaching staff. They may be attached to a particular school for a single day or even part of a day, or for a substantially longer period.

Peripatetic teacher
Some qualified teachers are not attached to a particular school but visit and work in several schools in an area, for instance teaching music or languages, or working with partially hearing children.

Home liaison teacher
In some LEAs there are qualified teachers whose job is to liaise between the school and the home, by visiting the child's family at home, seeing parents if they visit the school, and by organising activities, both during and after school hours, to encourage parental involvement with the school and with their children's education. They are most likely to be attached to primary schools in areas of social need, or to special schools.

Educational home visitor
Some LEAs employ teachers to visit families with preschool children before they start school, usually for about an hour a week, to play with the children and involve the parents in finding out more about the children's development and needs. They perform a similar role to home liaison teachers in encouraging parental involvement in their children's education, but differ in working with children under five.

Home tutor
A home tutor is a teacher employed to teach children at home when they are unable to attend school for any length of time, for instance because of illness.

Laboratory technician/assistant
Laboratory technicians and assistants maintain laboratory and workshop equipment, usually in secondary schools or institutes of further or higher education. They provide technical assistance to teachers, especially in science subjects, and sometimes also deal with audio-visual equipment.

Audio-visual technician
Audio-visual technicians are responsible for the operation and maintenance of audio-visual equipment. Some posts exist attached to a particular secondary school, especially a very large comprehensive, but most A-V technicians are appointed to a local authority centre, or work in further or higher education.

Media resources officer
A few large authorities have created these posts, which involve not merely the operation and maintenance of audio-visual equipment and other educational technology, but also the preparation and production of audio-visual materials and the in-service training of teaching staff in the use of the equipment.

Ancillary staff

All educational establishments are dependent for their day-to-day running on the ancillary staff. They include the administrative and clerical staff, who often work part-time, especially in primary schools: the secretaries, clerical assistants, typists, and (especially in private boarding schools) bursars, who are responsible for the school's financial and domestic management. Another group are the kitchen and canteen staff, responsible for providing school dinners. The other main category of ancillary staff can be described as premises-related: they include caretakers, cleaners, porters, gardeners and security staff.

(C) THE TEACHING PROFESSION

Salaries and conditions

The 1991 School Teachers' Pay and Conditions Act established a review body, its members appointed by the government, to make annual recommendations to the Secretary of State for Education about teachers' salaries and conditions of employment in England and Wales. Final decisions are then made by the Secretary of State, after consultation with LEAs, teachers' representatives and other interested parties, and set out in a School Teachers' Pay and Conditions Document.

The current salary structure (from September 1999 for heads and April 1999 for all other teachers) consists of a single 'spine' for all qualified teachers (apart from heads and deputy heads), of 35 points and 'half-points' from £13,830 to £37,041. Heads' and deputy heads' salaries range on two separate spines of 34 points from £31,155 to £70,002 for heads and £27,258 to £44,841 for deputies. These figures represent a salary increase of between 5% and 9.5% for heads, and 3.5% for other teachers.

The School Teachers' Pay and Conditions Documents spell out explicitly and exhaustively the duties, and the working time, of teachers at all levels. The duties include the following. Teachers are required to plan and prepare lessons, assess and keep records of pupils' progress, and maintain discipline. They are to engage in appraisal of their own work, and attend in-service training. They must communicate with parents and others outside school, and attend meetings where necessary. They must provide cover for absent colleagues for up to three days, though this can be extended for a teacher whose assigned duties occupy less than three-quarters of his or her working week, or where the school authorities have 'exhausted all reasonable means' but failed to provide a supply teacher to replace the absent colleague. Finally, they must participate, when required, in the appraisal of other teachers' performance.

A teacher's working year is to consist of 1265 hours, spread reasonably over 195 working days. (This does not include travelling time to and from school.) In addition, teachers must work such extra hours as are needed to fulfil their professional duties, for example in preparing lessons and marking pupils' written work. Teachers are entitled to a reasonable midday break, and do not have to supervise pupils during this period as part of their normal duties (DfEE, 1997, Part XI).

Under proposals introduced for consultation by the Government in December 1998 and February 1999, a new system of appraisal-linked pay is to be introduced. All teachers will be appraised annually by senior managers at their school (with review by external assessors drawn from a pool of 'nationally trained experts'). On the basis of this appraisal, head teachers will make recommendations to governing bodies about each teacher's pay. Heads will themselves be appraised by governing bodies, assisted by independent advisers, and the governing bodies will take this into account in setting the level of the heads' pay. The separate heads' and deputy heads' spines will be replaced by a single *Leadership Spine*, covering not only heads and deputies, but other teachers with senior management responsibilities, and also *Advanced Skills Teachers*, teachers of exceptional ability who will be able to attain high levels of pay without leaving classroom teaching.

F A C T   Approximately 498,000 full-time teachers were employed in schools in the UK in 1993–4 (1% below the number employed in 1990–1, and 12% below the number employed in 1980–1). Of these, 91% taught in maintained schools (45% in secondary, 43% in primary and 3% in special schools) and the remaining 9% taught in the private sector (GSS, 1996, Table 9).

Women outnumber men in the teaching profession, making up over three-quarters of the teachers in primary schools, and just under half of the teachers in secondary schools. They are particularly highly represented as teachers of the youngest children. Figure 7.2 shows that as the age of the pupil increases, so the proportion of women teachers decreases.

29% of male teachers in primary schools and 28% of male teachers in secondary schools are on the lowest quarter of the salary 'spine'; the corresponding figures for female teachers are 48% (primary) and 34% (secondary). At the other end of the scale, 47% of all male teachers in primary schools are heads or deputy heads, as are 9% of all male teachers in secondary schools; the corresponding figures for female teachers are 21% and 6% (1995–6 figures, DfEE, 1997, Table 24).

Ethnic minorities appear to be under-represented in the teaching profession in comparison with their numbers in the population, though the evidence is not up to date. In eight LEAs surveyed in 1987 by the Commission for Racial

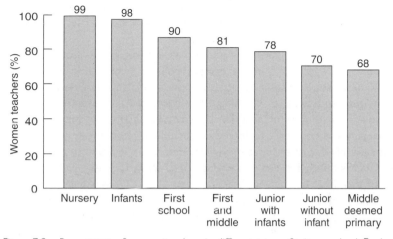

Figure 7.2   Percentages of women teachers in different types of primary school, England and Wales 1990
(Adapted from DES, no date, Table B12/90)

Equality, the overall percentages of teachers who were from ethnic minorities was 2% (Ranger, 1988); the percentage of the total population of these LEAs who are from ethnic minorities is about 8.5% (OPCS, 1982). However the latter figure is based on answers to a question in the 1981 Census about the country of birth of one's head of household, and cannot be considered very accurate (see Chapter 2).

Teachers from ethnic minorities were more likely to be found in junior posts than White teachers: in 1987 (under a different system of salary scales), 78% of ethnic minority teachers were on the lowest two scales, compared with 57% of White teachers. Ethnic minority teachers were twice as likely as White teachers to be teaching subjects in which there is a shortage of teachers (Ranger, 1988).

Training and qualifications

There are at present two main ways of becoming a qualified teacher in England and Wales: by taking an undergraduate course of initial teacher training – usually lasting four years and leading to a BEd degree; or, for graduates or the holders of equivalent qualifications in an appropriate subject, a postgraduate course of initial teacher training – usually lasting one year and leading to a Postgraduate Certificate in Education (PGCE). There are also some part-time PGCE courses, normally lasting two years.

In addition, LEAs and governing bodies can employ *licensed teachers*. These must be over 24 years old, and have successfully completed at least two years of full-time higher education (or its part-time equivalent), but need not have had any teacher training or teaching experience. The employer must provide 'tailor-made, on-the-job training' for such teachers, who can obtain qualified teacher status in two years or less. *Overseas trained teachers* can be employed, and gain qualified teacher status in England and Wales, in a similar way.

Since 1994, teacher training in England and Wales has been under the auspices of the Teacher Training Agency (TTA). The TTA was established with the aim of increasing the involvement of schools in both the initial and the in-service training of teachers (see Chapter 4: 1994 Education Act).

Teacher training in Northern Ireland and Scotland follows a pattern similar to that in England and Wales. However, in Scotland there are separate courses for primary and secondary teachers, and the Teaching Qualification (Primary Education) and the Teaching Qualification (Secondary Education) are distinct, making it more difficult for teachers in Scotland to move between the two sectors than in the rest of the United Kingdom (Marker, 1994, Section 15).

In 1994–5, a total of 73,400 students were enrolled on initial teacher training courses in the United Kingdom in universities or colleges (see Figure 7.3). The proportion of the teaching force who have degrees has been steadily increasing (see Figure 7.4). It is higher among men than women, with the lowest proportion of graduates teaching in primary schools and the highest in non-maintained schools (see Figure 7.5).

An important aspect of the teacher's job is the size of the class he or she is expected to teach (on average, this is greater than the pupil/teacher ratio, as calculations of the latter include staff who do little or no classroom teaching). Primary classes are generally larger than classes in secondary schools. (For data on the pupil/teacher ratio, see Chapter 5; Figures 5.8 and 5.12.)

(D) TEACHING STAFF IN FURTHER AND HIGHER EDUCATION

> **F A C T**   In 1995–6, 66,500 academic staff were employed in further education colleges, and 59,700 in higher education (DfEE/OFSTED, 1998, Annexes P and Q).

Men far outnumber women in further and higher education teaching, especially in senior posts. In 1992–3, there were over three men to every woman at

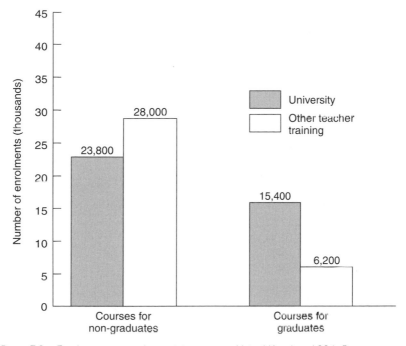

Figure 7.3   Enrolments on teacher training courses, United Kingdom 1994–5 (Adapted from GSS, 1996, Table 8)

lecturer level, almost nine men to every woman at senior lecturer level, and just over 19 men to every woman at the level of professor in British universities (see Figure 7.6). The discrepancy is particularly great in the sciences and mathematics, where male lecturers outnumber female by seven to one, and male professors outnumber female by 53 to one. However, the discrepancy between the sexes, though still huge, is currently decreasing. Women constituted 16% of all teaching staff in 1992–3, compared with 13% in 1988–9; and 5% of professors in 1992–3, compared with 3% in 1988–9.

Career structure

Until 1998 most academic teaching posts in universities were offered on a 'tenured' basis, so that academic staff could lose their jobs only on grounds of professional misconduct (and not on such grounds as redundancy or financial exigency). However, under the 1988 Education Reform Act no new tenured appointments can be made. Academics already in post retained their tenure

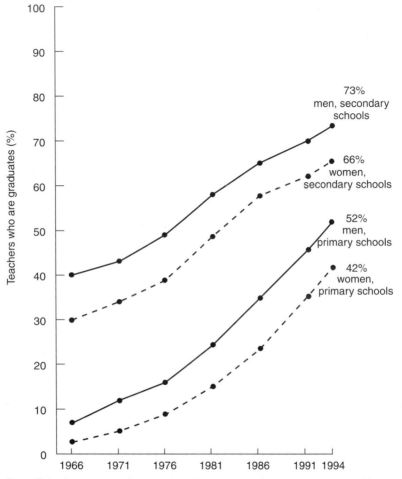

Figure 7.4 Percentages of men and women teachers who are graduates, in public sector primary and secondary schools, United Kingdom 1966–94
(Adapted from GSS, 1996, Table 9)

only so long as they did not move to another university or accept promotion within their present university.

The main traditional academic posts within universities are typically as described below, though there is a great deal of variation between universities, especially after the sudden expansion of the university sector following the 1992 Further and Higher Education Act.

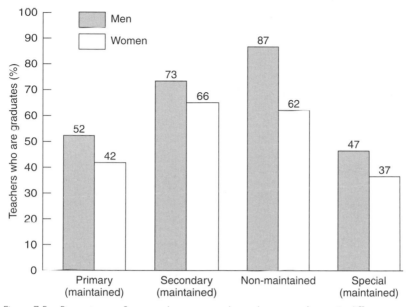

Figure 7.5   Percentages of men and women teachers who are graduates, in different types of school, United Kingdom 1993–4
Note: The Primary columns include nursery schools
(Adapted from GSS, 1996, Table 9)

Chancellor

The chancellor is the titular head of a university, with a purely ceremonial function, notably in conferring degrees. He or she is usually a well-known public figure, who need not have any connection with the academic world (such as a member of the Royal Family). In the ancient Scottish universities, the chancellor is elected by the graduates.

Pro chancellor

Nominally a deputy to the chancellor (for whom he or she sometimes stands in on ceremonial occasions, such as graduation ceremonies), the pro chancellor does have a substantial role, as chair of the council of a university, with overall responsibility for its financial and other non-academic affairs. It is usually a part-time appointment, often held by people distinguished in the world outside university, such as lawyers and business people.

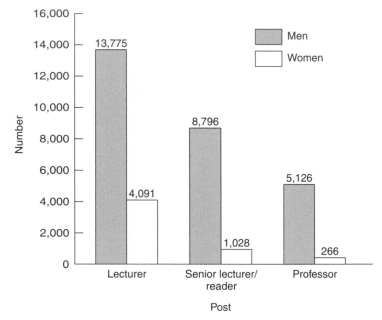

*Figure 7.6   Numbers of men and women teaching staff in universities, Great Britain 1992–3
(Adapted from Universities' Statistical Record, 1993, Vol. 1, Table 28)
Note: the former polytechnics and colleges are not included*

Vice chancellor (VC)

Again, the vice chancellor is nominally a deputy to the chancellor, but in reality is the chief academic and administrative officer of a university, in charge of its day-to-day running (though he or she also stands in for the chancellor on ceremonial occasions). He or she controls and coordinates the activities of committees and planning boards, oversees the working of academic departments and liaises with outside bodies. This is a full-time appointment, and in most universities a permanent one, though some (notably Oxford, Cambridge and London) elect their vice-chancellors for a period of several years at a time.

Principal

The chief academic and administrative officer of a Scottish university, he or she is usually styled 'principal and vice chancellor', the latter title used when standing in for the chancellor on ceremonial occasions. (The University of London has both a principal and a vice chancellor.)

Pro vice chancellor

Some universities now have deputy or pro vice chancellors, who chair major committees and stand in for the vice chancellors. These posts are often held for a limited term by senior academic members of the university.

Rector

A rector is the chair of the university court (the supreme decision-making body) of one of the ancient Scottish universities. Elected by the students for a term of several years, rectors have been less exclusively drawn than most other senior officers of universities from 'establishment' circles: they have included a communist trade union leader and several television personalities, such as Malcolm Muggeridge, John Cleese and Muriel Gray. Most treat the position as purely ceremonial, but they can actively preside over their courts' proceedings if they choose, and in recent years a number have done so. However the Garrick Committee (see Chapter 3: 1997 Garrick) has argued that this situation is 'too haphazard', and that the link between the rectorship and the chair of the court should be ended.

Master

A traditional title for the head of a college in Oxford and Cambridge Universities (and occasionally elsewhere).

Dean

A dean is the head of a faculty, such as a faculty of science, or a faculty of arts. A deanship may be a permanent appointment, or a temporary one held for a limited term by senior academic members of the faculty. The duties and powers of deans vary from university to university.

Professor

This is the highest purely academic appointment. Professors are responsible for conducting and promoting teaching and research in their subjects. A post as professor – known for historical reasons as a 'chair' – may be *established* or *personal*. An established chair is a permanent post in a university: when one occupant leaves it, another will normally be appointed in his or her place. A personal chair is conferred on a particular individual, traditionally for distinguished scholarship, research and published work (but now sometimes to mark administrative or managerial responsibilities), and continues only as long as his or her academic career. Traditionally, professors were the heads of academic departments. Often they still are, but in recent years it has become common for other senior academics to act as heads of departments, sometimes in rotation.

Reader

A reader engages in teaching and research. Like a personal chair, a readership is usually conferred on an individual for merit in scholarship, research and published work. In status, it lies between a professorship and a senior lectureship, but is equivalent to the latter in duties (and salary scale).

Senior lecturer

A senior lecturer engages in teaching and research. The criteria for promotion from lecturer are not clearly defined, but are generally concerned with qualities in teaching, research and, sometimes, administration. There is no sharp division of duties between senior lecturer and lecturer, but a senior lecturer is, in general, more likely than a lecturer to hold a post such as dean or head of department, or to chair university committees.

Lecturer

Lecturers engage in teaching and research. Despite their title, lecturers' teaching does not consist only, or even mainly, of giving lectures. They also hold tutorials and seminars, and comment on students' written work, as well as setting and marking examinations. (Lecturers at the Open University do not normally give lectures at all; they produce correspondence material for their students, as well as working with BBC colleagues on the production of radio and television programmes.) Most universities have no formal qualifications for the post of lecturer, but in practice, lecturers almost always have a good honours degree, and usually a higher degree and research experience. However, the Dearing Committee (see Chapter 3: 1997 Dearing) has recommended that university teachers should have teaching training and qualifications.

In addition, there are sometimes temporary posts such as 'teaching fellow' or 'tutorial assistant', which are available for a limited period.

As well as the academic posts above, which carry responsibilities for both teaching and research, universities also have posts with research duties alone. Research posts often have short-term contracts and are rarely held on a tenured basis. They are increasingly being funded by external sources, such as industry. Definitions of different levels of appointment are varied and sometimes imprecise, but two broad levels can be distinguished:

Research fellow or research officer

People who hold these posts are deemed able to carry out research without supervision. They generally have a higher degree.

Research associates or research assistant

The work of research associates and assistants is carried out under supervision, sometimes as part of a research team. They are often allowed (and expected) to spend part of their time studying for a higher degree.

The former polytechnics had a similar, though not identical hierarchy of posts, though they were too recently established to have acquired the more colourful historic positions and titles of the universities. Now that they have acquired university status, however, many have adopted, or are adopting, some of the traditional university posts and job titles (such as vice chancellor and professor). At present, there is some confusion of nomenclature since some titles (for example, senior lecturer) have different meanings in the older universities and former polytechnics.

SOURCES AND FURTHER READING

CIPFA (no single date) *Financial Information Services*, Vol. 20, *Education*, London: CIPFA.

CIPFA (1991) *Local Government Trends 1990*, London: CIPFA.

CSO (1994) *Social Trends*, No. 24, London: HMSO.

DFE (1993) *Circular 7/93: Inspecting Schools: a guide to the inspection provisions of the Education (Schools) Act 1992 in England*, London: DFE.

DfEE (1997) *School Teachers' Pay and Conditions Document 1997*, London: HMSO.

DfEE/OFSTED (1998) *Departmental Report/The Government's Expenditure Plans 1998–99*, Cm 3910, London: The Stationery Office.

DfEE (1997) *Statistics of Education: Teachers: England and Wales*, London: The Stationery Office.

Gordon, P. and Lawton, D. (1984) *A Guide to English Educational Terms*, London: Batsford.

GSS (1996) *Educational Statistics for the United Kingdom 1995*, London: HMSO.

Marker, W. B. (1994) *The Scottish Education System*, Edinburgh: Open University Scottish Region.

House of Commons (1998) *New Appointment Hearing: the OFSTED Complaints Adjudicator* – Minutes of evidence to the Education and Employment Committee, 15 July 1998, London: The Stationery Office.

OPCS (1982) *Census 1981: County Reports*, London: HMSO.

Ranger, C. (1988) *Ethnic Minority Teachers*, London: Commission for Racial Equality.

Universities' Statistical Record (1993) *University Statistics 1992–93: Vol. 1: Students and Staff*, Cheltenham: Universities' Statistical Record.

Welsh Office/Office of Her Majesty's Chief Inspector of Schools in Wales (1998) *The Government's Expenditure Plans 1998–99: Departmental Report by the Welsh Office and the Office of Her Majesty's Chief Inspector of Schools in Wales*, Cm 3915, London: The Stationery Office.

The funding of education in Great Britain (though not in Northern Ireland: see below) is shared between central and local government, in a fairly similar manner from country to country. Here, we first outline the English system, and then note some of the more significant differences in Scotland, Wales and Northern Ireland. However, all of the latter will be changed fundamentally as devolved governments assume responsibility for education in these countries from 1999: see Chapter 6.

ENGLAND

PART I   WHERE THE MONEY COMES FROM
The financing of education is shared between central and local government. Most of central government's contribution is indirect, consisting of grants to local authorities. Its direct expenditure is mainly for further and higher education. The local authorities' educational expenditure is mainly on schools.

F A C T   In 1996–7, central government's direct expenditure on education in England was £8.2 billion, of which about 42% was for higher education, and 38% for further education. Local authorities' expenditure on education amounted to £18.5 billion, 76% of it on schools and approximately 9% on further education (DfEE and OFSTED, 1998, Annexe Bi).

After the 1988 Education Reform Act and the 1992 and 1993 Education Acts, the local authorities' share of educational expenditure has diminished and will probably continue to diminish, though it is impossible to predict by how much. Under the terms of the 1998 Act, further education and what used to be LEA-controlled higher education were removed entirely from the control of LEAs, and are financed directly by central government. The 1988 and 1993 Acts allowed schools to become 'grant-maintained' and similarly receive their funding directly from central government. By 1996–7, about 1,100 schools had acquired GM status, with a total annual budget of £240 million. However, the 1998 School Standards and Framework Act replaces the category of grant-maintained from 2000 with that of 'foundation' schools, and it is not yet evident what implications this will have for the numbers of schools opting out of LEA financing. (See the entries on these Acts in Chapter 4, and also Chapter 6.) In addition, the 1988 Act reduced the LEAs' control even over those educational functions and services that they continue to finance (see Local Management of Schools below).

In principle, the creation of City Technology Colleges, entirely independent of LEAs, also diminishes the LEAs' role in the financing of education. In practice, however, only 15 CTCs have been created, accounting for an estimated £54 million of public funds in 1996–7. The official projections for future spending suggest that the government does not anticipate a significant increase in the size of the CTC sector (DfEE and OFSTED, 1998, Annexe Bi).

The establishment of Education Action Zones (see Chapter 6) may also diminish the LEAs contribution if substantial numbers are approved in which an LEA does not play the leading role.

Local government finance

Since 1993, the local authorities' money comes from three main sources. The first is the local community, through the Council Tax, the level of which is set by each local authority (though subject to 'capping' by central government). The second is central government, mainly in the form of a Revenue Support Grant (RSG). The third lies somewhere in between local and national revenue: the National Non-domestic Rate (or 'uniform business rate'), the level of which is set nationally and the proceeds of which are pooled nationally and distributed to local authorities in proportion to their populations. A small amount of money is also raised through fees and other charges, but this income is insignificant as a proportion of expenditure in the education service, unlike other services such as housing.

> **F A C T**   Most local authority expenditure in England is financed by central government grants, an estimated 78% for 1998–9, of which 41% is Revenue Support Grant, 26% National Non-domestic Rate, and 10% grants for specific purposes. The remaining 22% has to be raised by local authorities themselves from Council Tax (DETR, 1998, Fig. 11c).

Each year, the government draws up a *Standard Spending Assessment* (SSA), setting out the amount of expenditure it considers that each authority will require in order to provide a standard level of services. This takes into account the particular needs of the authority: some areas will have particularly high numbers of old people, for instance, or underprivileged groups, or bad housing, which require higher spending for the same level of services. Then, taking into account the resources of the authority, and the revenue available to it from the National Non-domestic Rate, the government decides how much Revenue Support Grant it will give, and how much revenue it considers should be raised by the authority itself through Council Tax.

However, a local authority decides its own level of Council Tax: it is not committed to following the government's recommendation. Of all the main sources of finance, only the level of Council Tax is within the control of the local authorities. Thus, any decision by an authority to spend more or less on services than the government's assumed level will be reflected directly in the level of tax it has to set. This is intended to increase the accountability of local authorities to their electorate. Nevertheless, the Secretary of State for the Environment is empowered to 'cap' the tax levels set by local authorities whose levels of Council Tax he or she considers excessive.

Local management of schools

Under the terms of the 1988 Education Reform Act, the LEAs continue (subject to such constraints as Council Tax capping) to set the overall, authority-wide budget for schools under their control (known as the 'general schools budget'). But thereafter, the powers of LEAs are now greatly restricted.

First, they are required to distribute most of these funds (the 'aggregated schools budget') between schools strictly and even-handedly according to a formula, to be devised by each LEA but requiring approval by the DfEE. An acceptable formula is expected to make each school's 'budget share' depend mainly on the numbers of pupils in the school, but also to take into account such factors as the ages of the children, the subjects they are studying, and the numbers with special needs; and also perhaps the levels of social advantage and disadvantage in the community the school serves. The intention is that an LEA will not be able to favour particular schools, or to use the granting and with-holding of funds as a means of enforcing policies, or of promoting some educational practices and discouraging others (except to a marginal extent with some limited discretionary funds that can be kept outside the aggregated budget).

Secondly, the LEAs are required to delegate many of their responsibilities for the management and control of the schools' budget share, and for the appointment and dismissal of staff, to the governing bodies of the schools. The members of a governing body may in their turn delegate most of these responsibilities to the head teacher, or they may choose to discharge them themselves. In either case, decisions about spending priorities – e.g. on staffing as against computers, or educational visits as against redecoration – and about the hiring and firing of teachers, will now be made at the level of the school itself, not by the LEA.

This system, known as the Local Management of Schools (LMS), is intended to provide increased accountability, and therefore efficiency. A school's funding now depends above all on its pupil numbers, and open enrolment under the 1988 Act (see Chapter 4) allows parents much wider choice of school for their children to attend. Schools will therefore be liable to lose pupils and funds if they fail to satisfy parents. This, the government believes, will make schools more directly and effectively accountable to parents, and more responsive to their criticisms and wishes.

Capital expenditure

Spending by both central and local government is of two types: current and capital. Current expenditure covers day-to-day items such as salaries and services; capital expenditure covers items with a longer-term use, such as buildings and machinery. About 95% of central and local government's combined spending on schools in 1996–7 was current, and 5% capital (DfEE and OFSTED, 1998, Annexe Bii).

The amount that local authorities can raise and spend on capital items is subject to controls by central government. Here, too, a new system has recently been introduced, this time in the 1989 Local Government and Housing Act. Under this system, the government still controls the total capital expenditure of local authorities, but now allows the authorities almost complete freedom to decide their own priorities within that overall sum. Local authorities now have four main sources of funds for capital expenditure: *borrowing*, which is subject to approval by central government; *capital grants*, from central government, which will specify the purposes for which they are to be used, and the amount the local authority must itself contribute; *capital receipts*, from the sale of assets such as land and council houses, though the local authorities must first set aside 50% of these receipts (75% in the case of council house sales) towards repaying their debts; and *ordinary revenue* from the Council Tax, for which the government assumes the local authorities to be accountable to their voters (CIPFA, no single date, Chapter 3; HM Treasury, 1990, Chapter 21, paras. 4.8–4.10).

Funding of training

Since the merger of the Department for Education and the Employment Department in 1995, a single department has been responsible for both the education and the vocational and pre-vocational training of young people, whether in school, FE college or the workplace. From 1997–8, new funding arrangements have been introduced, which are intended to bring about greater uniformity in the funding of young people's training, wherever it takes place. Under these arrangements, payment is by results: 15–25% of the budget for training programmes is allocated on the basis of numbers of trainees beginning a programme, 45–55% on the basis of their retention during the programme, and 25–35% on the basis of outcomes (DfEE and OFSTED, 1998, p. 71).

In 1996–7, a total of £734 million was spent on *work-based training for young people*. This included the Modern Apprenticeship, National Traineeship and other smaller schemes, and was managed largely through Training and Enterprise Councils (TEC) (see Chapter 12). During this year, just under 250,000 young people began training, and 56,000 gained one or more NVQ. The cost per trainee was £3,000, and the cost per NVQ £6,700 (DfEE and OFSTED, 1998, Table 2.14).

Funding of further education

From 1993, the funding of further education was transferred from LEAs to central government, through the Further Education Funding Council (see Chapter 4: 1992 Further and Higher Education Act, and also Chapter 5). For 1996–7, the expenditure of the FEFC was £3.2 billion. (In previous years, about 94% of FEFC expenditure was current, 6% capital, but the DfEE annual report no longer shows this breakdown) (DfEE and OFSTED, 1998, Annexe Bi).

Funding of higher education

From 1993, the funding of higher education was unified with a unitary Higher Education Funding Council, funded by central government (see Chapter 4: 1992 Further and Higher Education Act, and also Chapter 5). For 1996–7, the expenditure of the HEFC was £3.4 billion. (In previous years, about 90% of this was current, and 10% capital expenditure, but the DfEE annual report no longer shows this breakdown) (DfEE and OFSTED, 1998, Annexe Bi).

Regardless of these administrative arrangements, institutions of higher education have received and continue to receive their money from two main sources: *direct funding* from central or local government, and *student fees*, which traditionally were covered by mandatory or discretionary grants from LEAs. During the 1990s, however, successive governments, Conservative and Labour, have altered the balance between these, to increase the proportion of funding covered by fees. The change is intended to improve the performance of HE institutions by making their funding depend more on their ability to attract students, in competition with one another. From 1998, students are expected to make a contribution of £1000 per annum towards the cost of their tuition.

Also during the 1990s, a system of loans was introduced to supplement maintenance grants for undergraduate students. Originally, the loans and grants were each to cover 50% of students' living costs, but from 1998–9, the balance is shifting away from grants and towards loans, which will eventually replace grants completely. The loans will be repayable by graduates, through the Inland Revenue, when their income reaches a given level (currently set at £10,000 per annum).

1998–9 is a transitional year, when the balance of grant and loan for new students is 25%/75%. (For existing students, parity of grant and loan will be maintained.)

Teacher training

In response to teacher shortages, the government has exempted students on postgraduate certificate of education (PGCE) courses from paying the contribution to tuition fees required of other students in higher education. The initial training of teachers (ITT) and some of their inservice training (INSET) are funded through the Teacher Training Agency (TTA) (see Chapter 7). In 1996–7, the government grant to the TTA for ITT was £196 million, for some 58,000 students. For INSET, the TTA has begun a new process of competitive bidding by higher education institutions for three-year contracts as course providers. The DfEE has allocated £25.8 million to the TTA for this scheme in 1997–8, its first year of operation (DfEE and OFSTED, 1998, pp. 29–30).

Unofficial parental contributions

In addition to their official funding, a number of schools receive cash payments and other gifts from parents of their pupils. These contributions are not shown in official statistics of educational expenditure, but in 1990 an attempt was made to quantify them by the *Mail on Sunday*, which commissioned a survey of a representative sample of primary schools by the National Foundation for Educational Research. Overall, the researchers estimated, parents contributed some £40 million per annum to primary schools in England and Wales. But this total sum was distributed very unevenly among the schools. At one extreme, 6% of primary schools received less than £1 per child, and a further 21% less than £5; at the other extreme, 3% of schools received over £50 per child and 0.2% over £100. (The highest figure found for an individual school was £248 per child.) In about 13% of schools, the money contributed by parents amounted to more than the schools' official funding from their LEAs.

Of this money, 18% was spent on computers – the largest single item of expenditure. A further 14% was spent on books, and other major items were educational visits, decoration and maintenance, science equipment and furniture (Lightfoot, 1990).

PART 2 WHERE THE MONEY GOES
Overall spending on education

Education is one of the largest consumers of public money: the total expenditure on education in 1996–7 by central and local government in England was an

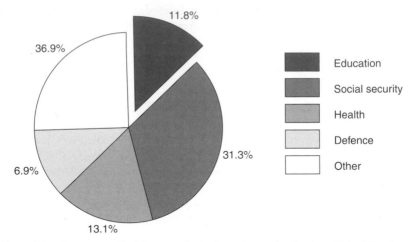

11.8%

36.9%

31.3%

6.9%

13.1%

- Education
- Social security
- Health
- Defence
- Other

Figure 8.1 Percentage of public expenditure devoted to major functions, United Kingdom, 1997–8
(Adapted from HM Treasury, 1998, Table 3.2)

estimated £29.5 billion, some 12% of the total spending on all services. Only Social Security and Health had more spent on them. Figure 8.1 shows public expenditure for 1996–7 on the highest spending services.

Within the education service, estimated expenditure in 1996–7 planned by the DfEE and LEAs is divided as shown in Figure 8.2.

Of the £18.5 billion (63%) spent on schools, nearly all (£17.5 billion) is current expenditure by LEAs. This is divided between sectors as shown in Figure 8.3.

By contrast, since the 1988 and 1992 Acts, most expenditure on further and higher education is current expenditure by central government, nearly all through the Further Education and Higher Education Funding Councils.

Taking all sectors together, LEA gross expenditure is divided among various categories as shown in Figure 8.4.

Trends over time in overall spending

Expenditure on education has increased fairly steadily over the last few years, in terms of money actually spent, though there has been a slight decline recently in 'real terms' after inflation is taken into account, as Figure 8.5 shows.

During the same period (1991–2 to 1996–7), general government spending on education fell from 12.4% to 11.8% of total government spending, and from 5.0% to 4.9% of GDP (HM Treasury, 1998, Tables 3.1 and 3.2).

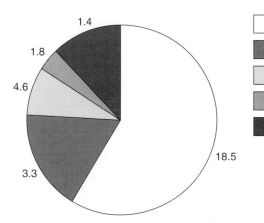

Figures in £ billions

Schools

Further education

Higher education

Student support in
FE and HE

Administration, inspection
and miscellaneous

*Figure 8.2 DfEE and English LEA spending 1996–7
(Adapted from DfEE and OFSTED, 1998, Annexe Bii)*

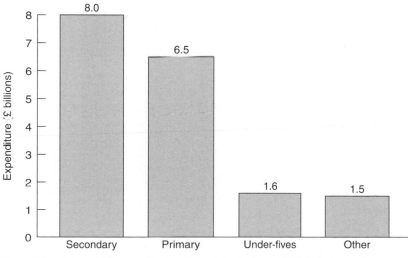

*Figure 8.3 Current LEA expenditure on schools in England, 1996–7 (estimated)
(Adapted from DfEE and OFSTED, 1998, Annexe Bii)*

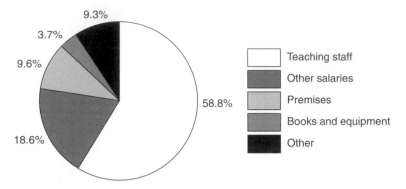

Figure 8.4   Percentage of LEA total gross expenditure in major categories, England and Wales, 1995–6
(Adapted from CIPFA, 1997, Figure 7)

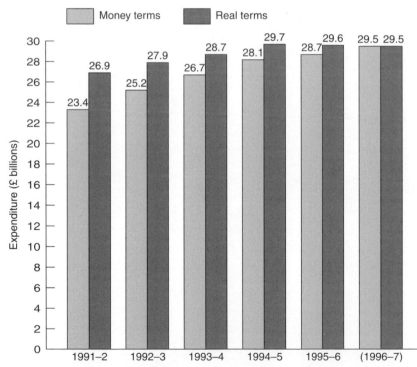

Figure 8.5   Total expenditure on education by central and local government, England, 1991–2 to 1996–7, in money terms and real terms
(Adapted from DfEE/OFSTED, 1998, Annexe Bii)
Note: The 'real terms' figures are expressed in 1996–7 values using official estimates of inflation; the 1996–7 figures are estimates

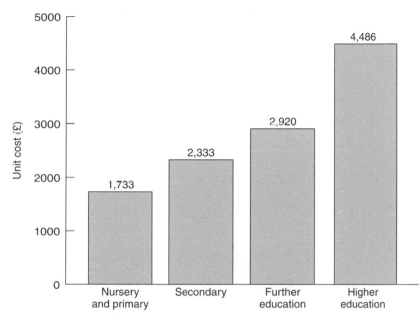

Figure 8.6   Unit costs (per pupil or student per annum) of education, England, 1996–7 (Adapted from DfEE/OFSTED, 1988, Tables 1.10 and 2.3, Annexes Bii and Q)

Expenditure per pupil or student

Educational expenditure is often expressed in terms of the amount spent per pupil or student. This figure is known as the 'unit cost', and is arrived at simply by dividing the total amount spent on a service (e.g. nursery schools) by the number of children using it (expressed as 'full-time equivalents', so that two part-time children could count as one full-time equivalent). Unit costs vary considerably between different sectors of the education system, as is shown by Figure 8.6.

Regional variations in expenditure per pupil

There is considerable variation between regions in the amount spent per pupil, as illustrated in Figure 8.7 for two sample ages (in mid-primary and mid-secondary respectively). Unit costs in London have been consistently higher than elsewhere. This is partly because of higher rates and premises costs and the London weighting in salaries, in addition to the extra demands placed on

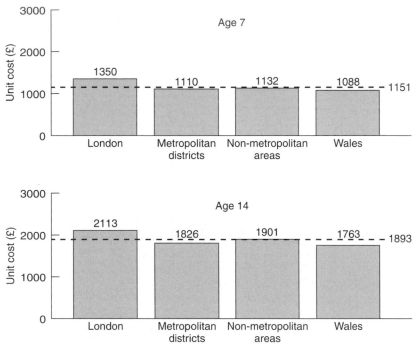

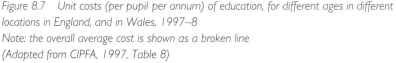

Figure 8.7   Unit costs (per pupil per annum) of education, for different ages in different locations in England, and in Wales, 1997–8
Note: the overall average cost is shown as a broken line
(Adapted from CIPFA, 1997, Table 8)

the education service by inner-city characteristics, such as high unemployment, widespread poverty and a greater diversity of cultures and languages.

There are also regional variations in the proportions of the unit cost that is spent on different items. Figure 8.8 shows the range of spending on books and equipment.

Trends over time in unit costs

Unit costs for LEA-maintained schools have fallen slightly in real terms in the 1990s. Taking all schools and all items of expenditure together, the 1996–7 unit costs were 97% of those in 1991–2. However, this overall figure masks a rise in the unit costs of nursery and primary schools (of 2%) and a larger fall in that of secondary schools (of 6%).

Units costs may be broken down into the amounts spent on different items

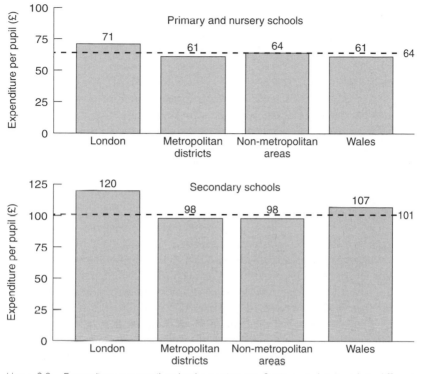

Figure 8.8   Expenditure per pupil on books, equipment, furniture and materials in different locations in England, and in Wales, 1995–6
Note: the overall average cost is shown as a broken line
(Adapted from CIPFA, 1997, pp. 74 and 76)

of expenditure, which do not always change at the same rate. Thus the spending per pupil on teaching staff (the largest single item of expenditure) was the same in 1996–7 as in 1991–2, as was that on books and equipment. During the same period, however, spending per pupil on support staff rose by 42%, and spending per pupil on repairs and maintenance fell by 21% (DfEE and OFSTED, 1998, Tables 1.10 and 1.11).

In the same period, unit costs in further and higher education fell more substantially – in FE by 12% and in HE by 15%. This has arisen from a substantial increase in student numbers without a commensurate increase in funding or staffing (DfEE and OFSTED, 1998, Tables 2.3 and 2.6).

Pupil/teacher ratio and class size

Another measure of the resources available in education is the pupil/teacher ratio (PTR), calculated by dividing the number of pupils by the number of qualified teachers or full-time teacher equivalents. It is lower in private than in maintained schools (i.e. there are fewer pupils per teacher), and it is lowest of all in special schools. As schools rolls have declined, the PTR has fallen.

Although the PTR is the measure on which decisions about resource allocation are often based, it is the size of the class as taught which has greater implications for children's learning experience. Class sizes are generally larger than PTRs, because not all teachers actually teach (heads, for instance, spend most or all of their time on administrative work), because marking and preparation duties restrict direct contact hours with pupils, and because sometimes classes are combined or split up for various periods.

Changes over time, and variations between different countries of the United Kingdom in PTRs are illustrated in Chapter 5 (see especially Figures 5.8 and 5.12). There is also variation between LEAs. For example, the PTR in English primary schools in 1998 varied from just over 18 to 1 in the London Borough of Kensington and Chelsea to 26 to 1 or more in Derbyshire, Hartlepool, Hull and the East Riding of Yorkshire. And the PTR in English secondary schools in 1998 varied from 13 to 1 in the London Borough of Kensington and Chelsea to over 19 to 1 in North East Lincolnshire and Northumberland. (The very lowest PTRs of any English LEA were in the Isles of Scilly and the City of London, but they had only around 300 and 200 pupils respectively in total (DfEE, 1998).)

School meals

In 1980, responsibility for the provision of school meals passed from central government to the LEAs. They were initially required to provide free meals for children in families receiving Supplementary Benefit, and to provide a place for children to eat food they brought from home, but otherwise the level, type and price of provision, if any, was left to the discretion of the individual LEA. By 1986, however, all obligations on LEAs to provide meals were removed, and their powers to supply free meals reduced. (See Chapter 4: 1980 Education Act; 1986 Social Security Act.) Most authorities now operate a cafeteria system in secondary schools, although a fixed-price system is still more common in primary schools, and some authorities provide no canteen facilities at all. Fewer than half of the pupils in maintained schools take school meals, with the rest bringing their own food or making other arrangements – mostly going home for lunch. (See Figure 8.9.)

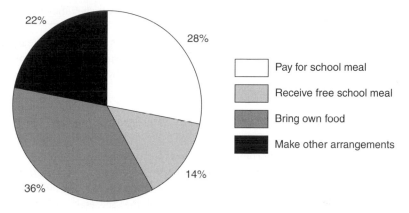

Figure 8.9   Types of meals at school, maintained schools, England, January 1992 (Adapted from DFE, 1993, Table A14/92)

SCOTLAND

Until the new, devolved government takes over from mid-1999, expenditure on education in Scotland is the responsibility, directly or indirectly (through influence on local authorities), of the Secretary of State for Scotland. Together with such services as health, roads and transport, law and order and housing, it falls within a category of spending programmes known as the Scottish Block. The Block comprised nearly 96% of all expenditure within the Secretary of State's responsibility in 1996–7. (The remaining 4%, though formally within his responsibility too, was in practice for programmes determined by United Kingdom or European Community policies.) The total Scottish Block is calculated each year by simply adopting the changes in expenditure agreed for comparable programmes in England, adjusted for the differences in population.

The Secretary of State then decides how to distribute this total among individual services. In 1996–7, total expenditure in the Scottish Block was £13.7 billion. Of this, £1.3 billion was allocated to the central government's (i.e. the Scottish Office's) own direct expenditure on education. But this sum – about 10% of the Block – represents only part of spending from the Block on education in Scotland, mostly on higher education. The rest, mostly on schools, comes from it to education in the shape of the funds allocated by the Secretary of State to local authorities, mainly through the Revenue Support Grant and the distribution of money raised from non-domestic rates: a total of £5.9 billion in 1996–7. The local authorities decide how to distribute this money among the various services they provide – together with the money they themselves raise from Council Tax. In 1996–7, the local authorities spent a total of £7.3 billion, of which 37% was on education (Scottish Office/Forestry Commission, 1998, Table 1.1; Appendices 1 and 2).

At central government level, only health was a higher spender than education (though this ignores the spending in Scotland of the UK Department of Social Security). At local government level, education is by far the biggest single item of expenditure.

WALES

Until the new devolved government takes over from mid-1999, expenditure on education in Wales is the responsibility, directly or indirectly (through influence on local authorities) of the Secretary of State for Wales. As in Scotland, the expenditure nominally under the control of the Secretary of State for Wales is partly determined by United Kingdom and European Union policies (just over 4% in 1996–7, mainly on agriculture, fisheries and food), but mostly (96%, known as the Welsh Office Block) more genuinely under his or her control. The total Welsh Office Block, and its distribution among the different services, are calculated each year by simply adopting the changes in expenditure agreed for comparable programmes in England, adjusted for the differences in population.

In 1996–7, total expenditure in the Welsh Office Block was £6.5 billion, of which £574 million was allocated to the Welsh Office's direct spending on education, Welsh language, arts and recreation. But this represents only part of spending from the Block on education in Wales. Much more money comes from it to education as funds allocated by the Secretary of State to local authorities, mainly through the Revenue Support Grant and the distribution of money raised from non-domestic rates: a total of £3.0 billion in 1996–7. The local authorities decide how to distribute this money among the various services they provide – together with the money they themselves raise from Council Tax. In 1996–7, the local authorities spent a total of £3.7 billion, of which 36% was on education, arts and libraries (Welsh Office/OHMCI, 1998, Tables 1.02 and 5.02). At central government level, only health was a higher spender (though this ignores the spending in Wales of the Department of Social Security). At local government level, education is by far the biggest single item of expenditure.

NORTHERN IRELAND

Until the new devolved government takes over in 1999 (subject to negotiations still in progress as we go to press), educational spending in Northern Ireland is the responsibility of the Secretary of State for Northern Ireland. As with public expenditure in Great Britain, the total Northern Ireland public expenditure and its division between services are announced in the

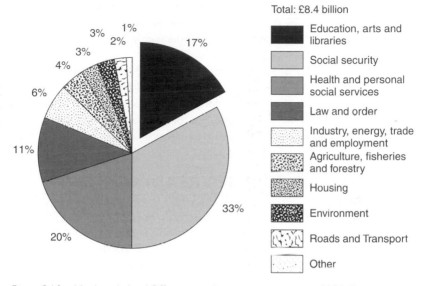

Figure 8.10   Northern Ireland Office expenditure on major services, 1996–7
(Adapted from Northern Ireland Office Department of Finance and Personnel/HM
Treasury, 1998, Chart 1.2)
Note: Expenditure on law and order does not include that on the army in Northern Ireland

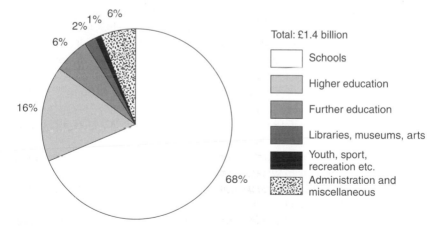

Figure 8.11   Expenditure by DFNI (including that by Education and Library Boards) on
main groups of services, 1997–8 (estimated)
(Adapted from Northern Ireland Department of Finance and Personnel/HM Treasury,
1998, Table 7.1)

government's annual expenditure plans. For 1998–9, planned expenditure on the major services was as shown in Figure 8.10. As in the rest of the United Kingdom, education is one of the highest spenders; only health and social security spend more.

Unlike those in the rest of the United Kingdom, Northern Ireland's local educational authorities, the Education and Library Boards, receive all their funding from central government, here, the Department of Education Northern Ireland (DENI). The percentages of the total expenditure of the DENI and boards allocated to their five main groups of services are shown in Figure 8.11.

SOURCES AND FURTHER READING

CIPFA (no single date) *Financial Information Services*, Vol. 20, London: CIPFA.

CIPFA (1989) *Education Statistics: 1989–90 Estimates*, London: CIPFA.

CIPFA (1990) *Handbook of Education Unit Costs 1987/88*, London: CIPFA.

CIPFA (1997) *Education Statistics: 1995–96 Actuals, incorporating the Handbook of Unit Costs*, London: CIPFA.

DETR (1998) *Annual Report 1998/The Government's Expenditure Plans 1998–99*, Cm 3906, London: The Stationery Office.

DFE (1993) *Statistics of Schools 1992*, London, DFE.

DfEE (1998) *DfEE News: Pupil/teacher ratios in maintained schools in England*, London: DfEE.

DfEE and OFSTED (1998) *Departmental Report/The Government's Expenditure Plans 1998–99*, Cm 3916, London: The Stationery Office.

Department of the Environment (1994) *Annual Report 1994/The Government's Expenditure Plans 1994–95 to 1996–97*, Cm 2507, London: HMSO.

Department of Finance and Personnel (Northern Ireland Office)/HM Treasury (1998) *Northern Ireland Expenditure Plans and Priorities: The Government's Expenditure Plans 1998–99*, Cm 3916, London: HMSO.

EDG (1994) *Departmental Report: The Government's Expenditure Plans 1994–95 to 1996–97*, Cm 2505, London: HMSO.

HM Treasury (1990) *The Government's Expenditure Plans 1990–91 to 1992–93*, London: HMSO.

HM Treasury (1994) *Public Expenditure: Statistical Supplement to the Financial Statement and Budget Report 1994–95*, Cm 2519, London: HMSO.

HM Treasury (1998) *Public Expenditure: statistical analyses 1998–99*, Cm 3901, London: The Stationery Office.

Lightfoot, L. (1990) 'Scandal of our schools', *The Mail on Sunday*, 27 May 1990, pp. 1–2.

Northern Ireland Office Department of Finance and Personnel/HM Treasury (1998) *Northern Ireland Expenditure Plans and Priorities: The Government's Expenditure Plans 1998–99*, Cm 3916, London: The Stationery Office.

Scottish Office/Forestry Commission (1998) *Serving Scotland's Needs: the Government's Expenditure Plans 1998–99*, Cm 3914, Edinburgh: The Stationery Office.

Welsh Office/OHMCI (1998) *The Government's Expenditure Plans 1998–99: a report by the Welsh Office and the Office of Her Majesty's Chief Inspector of Schools in Wales*, Cm 3915, London: The Stationery Office.

Qualifications are of many different kinds and levels. Some are predominantly academic, others vocational. Some are normally obtained through study at school, some through further or higher education, and some at the workplace. Courses outside school leading to qualifications up to and including A level or its equivalent are defined as *further education* (FE); those leading to qualifications above A-level standard as *higher education* (HE).

Many have undergone substantial change in recent years, and more changes are likely in the near future. In March 1996, Sir Ron Dearing, the then chairman of the School Curriculum and Assessment Authority, completed an inquiry on behalf of the Government into the education and training of young people aged 16–19 in England and Wales. (See Chapter 3: 1996 Dearing.) Both the Conservative government in office when Dearing reported and its Labour successor were generally favourable to the Dearing proposals, and some were implemented quickly, notably the unification of the bodies responsible in England for academic education and for vocational and pre-vocational training to form the Qualifications and Curriculum Authority (QCA). The parallel bodies in Scotland were also unified as the Scottish Qualifications Authority (SQA), and similar dual responsibilities were assigned to the Qualifications, Curriculum and Assessment Authority for Wales (ACCAC) and the Northern Ireland Council for the Curriculum, Examinations and Assessment (CCEA).

However, the new Government decided to hold consultations before implementing most of the other Dearing recommendations. A consultation document was issued in October 1997 (DfEE, 1997), and the Government announced its response to the replies in April 1998. Its own main proposals, mostly to be implemented from September 2000, are listed below, and some of the others noted in the body of the present chapter.

- A levels will be retained, in both their traditional 'linear' and their newer 'modular' forms, and present standards upheld, but regulations concerning the modular form will be tightened. All candidates will be examined on their understanding of the syllabus as a whole, and only one resit per module will be permitted. The coursework component will be restricted to 25–30% of the total marks.
- AS levels (renamed 'Advanced Subsidiary') will be revised to correspond to the first year of a full A level course. This will allow students to study up to five subjects to AS level, rather than making a choice of three A level subjects in their first year after GCSE. It will also enable them to leave open the decision of whether to proceed to full A levels, or complete their studies at AS level.
- Advanced GNVQs will be expanded: as well as a full 12-unit GNVQ (equivalent to two A levels), there will be from September 2000 a six-unit GNVQ

- (equivalent to one A level) and provisionally from September 2001 a three-unit GNVQ (equivalent to one AS level). Arrangements will be made to allow GNVQs to be combined with other vocational qualifications.
- A new, separate qualification in the 'key skills' of *communication, application of number* and *information technology* will be introduced in pilot form from September 1999. It will be assessed by a combination of coursework and external tests. (These key skills should continue to form part of GNVQ, and also be taught more widely as part of other academic and vocational courses, including A level and NVQ.)
- The QCA is asked to examine the possible development of an 'overarching' certificate (similar to the 'National Advanced Diploma' proposed by Dearing) to cover both A level and vocational results; and also to look more generally at the possibility of a unified, unit-based qualification framework covering academic and vocational studies.

The present chapter describes the position as we go to press in early 1999, before the implementation of these changes, but the most important of the proposed changes are mentioned.

SCHOOL AND FURTHER EDUCATION: ACADEMIC

GCSE (General Certificate of Secondary Education)

In 1986, GCSE courses were introduced to create a single examination system in England, Wales and Northern Ireland for those aged 16 or over (though younger pupils can be entered). GCSE is awarded on an 8-point scale (A*–G), with much emphasis originally placed on assessment of course work as well as a final examination, though the relative importance of the examination has been subsequently increased.

SCE (Scottish Certificate of Education) Standard grade

In 1984, the first SCE Standard grade courses were introduced in Scotland, with the first examinations in 1986. They are taken by all pupils, but with three levels of study and award (Foundation, General and Credit). Pupils receive a certificate at the end of their fourth year giving a 'profile' of their attainments (see Chapter 3, 1977 Dunning).

GCE (General Certificate of Education) A level

Introduced in 1951 in England, Wales and Northern Ireland, A levels are aimed at the most academically able pupils. Over 25% of 17-year-olds take two or more A levels, usually in full-time education in school, sixth-form college or FE college. They are widely used as entrance qualifications for higher education. Since 1994, a 'modular' A level has been available (in addition to the traditional form where students are assessed for the entire course at the same time). By 1997, a quarter of all A levels taken were modular.

SCE Higher grade

The SCE Higher is the Scottish alternative to the A level. Unlike A levels, Highers are taken one year after Standard grade rather than two years after GCSE, and over four or five subjects rather than two or three. They are normally taken between the ages of 16 and 18. In 1994, the government published proposals for the reform of the curriculum and assessment in the fifth and sixth years of Scottish secondary education (Scottish Office, 1994). These proposals were in response to the Report of the Howie Committee. The government accepted many of the committee's criticisms of current arrangements, but rejected its proposals for replacing them (see Chapter 3: Howie). Instead, Highers are to be retained, but as just one level in a five-level system of courses and qualifications being developed for fifth- and sixth-year pupils. The recommended study time for each Higher is to be increased from 120 to 160 hours. In addition, Advanced Higher courses are being developed, requiring 320 hours of study (and replacing the present CSYS: see below). The new system will operate from August 1999.

AS level (Advanced Supplementary)

This is an examination taken alongside A levels, involving about half the work of an A level, and aimed at broadening the curriculum. It has been available since September 1987, with the first examinations in summer 1989. As mentioned above, it is to be revised to correspond with the first year of an A level course, and to be renamed 'Advanced Subsidiary'.

CSYS (Certificate of Sixth Year Studies)

The CSYS is a qualification available to Scottish pupils after a year of study following Highers. It is to be replaced in 1999 by the Advanced Higher (see SCE Higher grade above).

SCHOOL AND FURTHER EDUCATION: PRE-VOCATIONAL AND VOCATIONAL

By the 1980s, there were about 6,000 different pre-vocational and vocational qualifications, awarded by about 600 different qualifying bodies (Rogers, 1988,

p. 26). In the late 1980s, the government began to rationalise these, and by the early 1990s it had decided to unify them in frameworks provided by the now replaced National Council for Vocational Qualifications (NCVQ) in England, Wales and Northern Ireland, and the Scottish Vocational Education Council (SCOTVEC). Even so, there are still some 3,000 qualifications eligible for public funding but not externally accredited (DfEE, 1997; for detailed information see the volume *British Vocational Qualifications* in the booklist at the end of this chapter). The main bodies awarding qualifications are listed below, with brief descriptions of the traditional qualifications they have offered and in some cases still offer. These are followed by descriptions of the newer qualifications frameworks devised by the NCVQ and SCOTVEC, which are to incorporate or replace many of them over the next few years.

RSA Examinations Board

An offshoot of the Royal Society of Arts, the RSA Examinations Board offers a range of qualifications for office and commercial work and languages. These can be taken on a full- or part-time basis, usually in FE colleges, but also in some schools. There are three stages of award: Elementary, Intermediate and Advanced.

London Chamber of Commerce and Industry (LCCI)

The LCCI offers a variety of qualifications in business, secretarial and language studies, again at three levels (Elementary, Intermediate and Higher).

City and Guilds of London Institute (CGLI)

The CGLI offers training and qualifications for most of the craft industries, offering over 200 subjects from hairdressing to engineering. Many job advertisements specify the precise City and Guilds Certificate required by number, e.g. CGLI 599 in construction services welding or CGLI 465 in tailoring. Three tiers of certificate are offered: Part 1, usually taken after one or two years' part-time study; Part 2 or Final Certificate after another two years; and a Part 3 or Advanced Certificate is available in some subjects, usually including some training for management. The CGLI is an independent body and the courses are drawn up by specialist committees including representatives from government, industry and teaching.

Edexcel

Formerly the Business and Technology Education Council (BTEC), Edexcel offers training for jobs in industry, commerce and administration. Each of the three levels of training (First, National and Higher National) can be taken as a

Certificate (usually two years part-time alongside employment) or as a Diploma (normally two years full-time or three years sandwich). The National qualifications are a vocational equivalent to academic A levels, the Higher National to ordinary degrees. These qualifications replace the Ordinary and Higher National Certificates and Diplomas (ONC/OND, HNC/HND) that preceded them.

Qualifications and Curriculum Agency (QCA)

The QCA was established in 1997, taking over responsibility for the work pre-viously carried out by the National Council for Vocational Qualifications (NCVQ), as well as that of the School Curriculum and Assessment Authority (SCAA). Like the NCVQ, the QCA is not an examining body itself, but moni-tors existing awarding bodies and their qualifications in England, Wales and Northern Ireland – approving those that meet certain standards, which it sets, and showing where they stand in relation to one another. Those it approves are designated National Vocational Qualifications (NVQ), or General National Vocational Qualifications (GNVQ). NVQs are intended mainly for people in work or in Youth Training. They are usually directed at specific occupations, and assessment normally takes place in workplace conditions. GNVQs are mainly for students aged 16–18 in full-time education, and, as their name sug-gests, directed at broad vocational areas rather than particular jobs, and uni-form throughout the country.

NVQs may be taken at five main levels:

- Foundation
- Basic craft
- Technician/Advanced craft/Supervisor
- Higher technician/Junior management
- Professional/Middle management

An Entry level was added from 1998 for those not yet ready for Foundation level.

GNVQs may be taken at three levels:

- Foundation (normally one year of full-time study)
- Intermediate (normally one year of full-time study after Foundation level)
- Advanced (normally two years of full-time study after Intermediate level)

And again, an Entry level was added from 1998, for those not yet ready for Foundation level.

GNVQs are awarded with pass, merit or distinction grades. They were intro-duced progressively from September 1993, and are now available in a wide range of vocational areas.

NVQ and GNVQ courses and qualifications may be combined with one another, and with GCE and GCSE courses and qualifications (DFE/Welsh Office, 1994; DFE/Welsh Office, no date).

Scottish Qualifications Agency (SQA)

The SQA was established in 1997, taking over responsibility for the work previously carried out by the Scottish Vocational Education Council (SCOTVEC) as well as that of the Scottish Examination Board (SEB). Since 1984, the SCOTVEC and now the SQA have offered a National Certificate and a Higher National Certificate, modular in structure, with students receiving credits for units of up to 40 hours' study. It was designed to be equivalent in standard to existing qualifications, such as those of the RSA and CGLI, and to replace them in Scotland. National Certificate courses can be taken in FE colleges, central institutions or secondary schools, and students can transfer between these institutions, or between them and other forms of training. Now the SQA also accredits and awards Scottish Vocational Qualifications (SVQ) and General Scottish Vocational Qualifications (GSVQ) – equivalent to NVQ and GNVQ in the rest of the United Kingdom (see above: Qualifications and Curriculum Agency).

COMPARING ACADEMIC AND VOCATIONAL QUALIFICATIONS

The government has taken the three GNVQ levels as the basis for specifying more general levels that apply across GNVQs, NVQs, GCSEs and GCE A and AS levels. These are:

Foundation Level

1 GNVQ at Foundation Level
or
1 NVQ at Level 1
or
4 GCSEs at grades D to G

Intermediate Level

1 GNVQ at Intermediate Level
or
1 NVQ at Level 2
or
5 GCSEs at grades A to C

Advanced Level

1 GNVQ at Advanced Level
or
1 NVQ at Level 3
or
2 GCE A levels *or* 4 AS levels *or* 1 A level plus 2 AS levels

Students or trainees are expected to attain Foundation level before proceeding to study at Intermediate level, and Intermediate level before studying at Advanced level. Advanced level qualifies for entry into Higher Education, or for advanced craft, technical, supervisory or administrative jobs (DFE/Welsh Office, 1994).

HIGHER EDUCATION

There is substantial variation among HE institutions in the qualifications they award, and in the meaning of apparently similar qualifications. To remove the resulting uncertainty and confusion, the Dearing Committee recommended the adoption of a uniform *National Qualifications Framework* (for details, see Chapter 3: 1997 Dearing). In response, the government accepted the principle of a uniform framework (for England, Wales and Northern Ireland, with a parallel framework for Scotland), but left the details to be agreed within the HE sector. The main elements of the framework are to be put in place by 2000. Here we describe the more complicated and less coherent position as we go to press in 1999.

Diploma in Higher Education (DipHE)

The DipHE is a qualification, validated where necessary by a university, that is gained after two years of study in a college of higher education. A qualification in its own right, it is, however, often now extended by further study to a degree. It was first introduced in 1974.

Professional awards

These are specialised qualifications necessary for working in particular professions, such as architecture, law and accountancy; they are awarded by the professional body concerned. (Relevant Edexcel diplomas and certificates sometimes count towards exemptions.)

Degree

Degrees are awarded by universities, colleges and institutes of higher education, and some FE colleges. Universities and some colleges (since 1998 known as 'university colleges') have the right to award their own degrees; degrees from other colleges have to be validated (that is, approved and underwritten) by a university. Normally a degree (apart from those of the Open University) requires three or four years' full-time study, but it may be taken as a four-year sandwich course, or in five to six years' part-time study. At the Open University, degree studies are part-time, and mainly by correspondence.

Degrees may be 'first degrees' or 'higher degrees' (see below). Most first degrees carry the title 'bachelor': Bachelor of Arts (BA), Bachelor of Science (BSc), Bachelor of Education (BEd), Bachelor of Engineering (BEng) and so on. At the four ancient Scottish universities, however, first degrees in arts faculties are generally called Master of Arts (MA), although the newer Scottish universities follow the English system and award bachelor degrees. Labels such as 'arts' or 'science' do not necessarily indicate the content of a course; some institutions award a BA in almost every discipline, including science and engineering.

Outside Scotland, first degrees are normally awarded at *honours* and *pass* levels, with honours degrees further divided into first class, second class (upper and lower) and third class. In Scotland, however, especially in the older universities, the alternative to an honours degree is not a 'pass' but an *ordinary* degree. This is not awarded to students on honours courses who fail to reach honours standard, but is a different type of degree, with less depth but often greater breadth (and requiring three years of study instead of four). It is traditionally a respected qualification in its own right (though less so than an honours degree), and is often a student's degree of choice (see Chapter 3: 1997 Garrick).

PGCE (Postgraduate Certificate in Education)

This is a one-year teacher-training qualification for those who already have a first degree. It is offered by universities and colleges of higher education.

Higher degree

Higher degrees are normally available only to those who already hold a first degree (especially a 'good' degree, i.e. with first-class or upper-second-class honours). Higher degrees are of two basic kinds – taught degrees (for which one normally sits an examination) and research degrees (for which one normally submits a thesis) – and of three basic levels.

The lowest level – usually, but not always, called 'master's' degrees – may be by either teaching or research, and may require one or two years of full-time study (or the equivalent in part-time study). There is no uniformity of terminology between institutions: such degrees include MA, MSc, MEd, MBA, MPhil, MLitt, etc. However the word 'master' does not always appear in the name of a postgraduate degree: BPhil, BLitt, LIB, BD and even sometimes BSc can be postgraduate degrees. Nor are all 'master's' degrees postgraduate: the four ancient Scottish universities call their first degree in arts an MA. Furthermore, a master's degree may not even be a qualification in the usual sense at all: Oxford and Cambridge University BA graduates can, after a specified number of years, obtain an MA without any further study or assessment.

The next level – usually called 'Doctor of Philosophy' (PhD or occasionally DPhil) regardless of the subject of study – normally requires the submission of a thesis based on original research, and is usually assumed to take three years of full-time study. Some institutions are now developing taught (rather than research-based) doctorates of equivalent level, with such titles as 'Doctor of Education' (EdD).

Finally, 'higher doctorates' (such as DSc, DLitt, DD) are awarded for distinguished contribution to an academic field, usually on the basis of books or other publications over a period of years.

Honorary degree

Awarded by universities according to any criteria they wish, honorary degrees are usually given as a mark of respect, congratulations or gratitude. They do not necessarily reflect or indicate any academic achievement. They normally take the form of higher degrees, occasionally master's degrees but more usually higher doctorates (Hon. DSc, Hon. LID, etc.); holders of honorary doctorates do not normally adopt the title 'Doctor'.

SOURCES AND FURTHER READING

Dearing, R. (1996) *Review of Qualifications for 16–19 Year Olds*, London: SCAA.

DfEE/OFSTED (1998) *Departmental Report: The Government's Expenditure Plans 1998–99*, Cm 3910, London: The Stationery Office.

DFE/Welsh Office (1994) *The New Qualifications Framework*, London: DFE.

DFE/Welsh Office (no date) *General National Vocational Qualifications: the new vocational A levels: a brief guide*, London: DFE.

DfEE (1997) *Qualifying for Success: a consultation paper on the future of post-16 qualifications*, London, DfEE.

ONS (1998) *Britain 1998: an official handbook*, London: The Stationery Office.

Rogers, R. (1988) A is for acronym, *School Governor*, No. 2, March.

Scottish Office (1994) *Higher Still: opportunity for all*, Edinburgh: Scottish Office.

(1996) *British Qualifications 27th Edition: a complete guide to educational, technical, professional and academic qualifications in Britain*, London: Kogan Page Ltd.

(1997) *British Vocational Qualifications: a directory of vocational qualifications available from all awarding bodies in Britain*, 2nd edn, London: Kogan Page Ltd.

The 1988 Education Reform Act introduced a compulsory curriculum into maintained schools in England and Wales, together with arrangements for assessing how it is being learnt. These provisions were extended, with modifications, to Northern Ireland, by the 1989 Education Reform (Northern Ireland) Order. This curriculum is to occupy most, but not all, of pupils' time during the years of compulsory schooling. Scotland does not have a statutory curriculum, but consistency between schools and regions of the country is achieved in other ways.

ENGLAND AND WALES

Before the 1988 Education Reform Act

For more than 40 years after the passage of the 1944 Education Act, central government had no formal role in determining the curriculum of schools. The 1944 Act specified only one compulsory subject – religious education – and even there individual pupils could opt out if their parents so wished. Otherwise, the curriculum was left formally to local education authorities, and in practice largely to headteachers – in association with governors after the 1986 Education Act (see Chapter 4).

In reality, of course, the structure and contents of school curricula during these years were subject to many constraints. These included such interrelated factors as GCE examination boards, university entrance requirements, HMI visits and reports, and the demands of parents. There was no single set pattern of subjects, but it would have been difficult for a school to neglect seriously those regarded as basic and normal. In 1984, four years before the introduction of the national curriculum, the percentages of time actually spent by the average pupil in England in the fourth and fifth year of secondary school (i.e. Years 10 and 11 in present-day terminology, and equivalent to Key Stage 4 as explained below) on what were to become the national curriculum subjects (or their nearest equivalents) were as shown in Figure 10.1.

The pattern of primary school curricula before 1988 is less well documented than that of secondary schools.

Introduction of the compulsory curriculum

The 1988 Education Reform Act, however, prescribed a compulsory *basic curriculum* for all maintained schools in England and Wales, which is to occupy most, but not necessarily all, of pupils' time. This has two components. First, the Act introduced a *national curriculum*, determined centrally by the government.

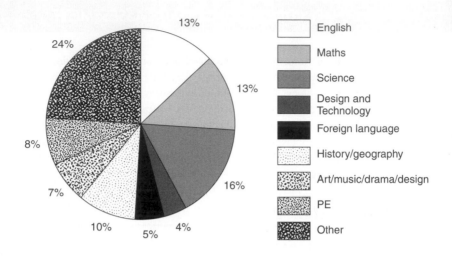

Figure 10.1   Percentage of time devoted to 'national curriculum subjects' by fourth and fifth year pupils, England, 1984
(Adapted from DES, 1987, Table 5)
Note: The national curriculum category of 'Design and Technology' was not used in the DES 1984 survey; the figure for 'Craft-based CDT' has been used here in its place.

Secondly, the 1988 Act, like the 1944 Education Act, made *religious education* compulsory, together with daily religious worship that would normally be 'broadly Christian' in character. Religious education is not part of the national curriculum, however: its syllabus is a matter for local agreement, not prescription by the central government, and parents may withdraw their children from it.

Since the 1993 Education Act, sex education (including education about HIV and AIDS) has a status similar to religious education, though in secondary schools only. It is compulsory for the schools to provide it, but it is outside the national curriculum and parents may withdraw their children from it. Sex education is required by the Act to have regard to moral considerations and the value of family life.

The government also proposes to introduce *careers education* as a compulsory subject outside the national curriculum in secondary schools.

The 1988 Act does not itself lay down in detail what the national curriculum should be, or how it should be assessed. Instead, it provides a skeleton structure, and empowers the Secretaries of State for Education and for Wales to fill in the details in ministerial orders. To assist the Secretaries of State in these decisions, there are now two statutory bodies, the Qualifications and

Curriculum Authority (QCA) (for England), and the Qualifications, Curriculum and Assessment Authority for Wales (ACCAC).

The national curriculum was subject to frequent modification in its early years, but more recently some stability has been achieved. The current ministerial orders in which the curriculum is set out have been in force since 1995, and the government does not plan to replace them until September 2000. (However, the compulsory requirements for some subjects at primary level were officially 'relaxed' in 1998: see below.)

The subjects of the national curriculum

The national curriculum is based on school *subjects*, some traditional, others new. In England, these subjects are as follows. (The first four, together with religious education, are officially designated 'core' and the rest 'foundation' subjects for the first two 'key stages' – see below.)

- English
- mathematics
- science
- information technology

- design and technology
- history
- geography
- music
- art
- physical education
- a modern foreign language

The requirements concerning these subjects vary according to the age of pupils. For the teaching and assessment of the national curriculum, the years of compulsory schooling are divided into four *key stages* (KS).

Key Stage 1 – up to age 7 (Years 1 and 2)
Key Stage 2 – up to age 11 (Years 3–6)
Key Stage 3 – up to age 14 (Years 7–9)
Key Stage 4 – up to age 16 (Years 10 and 11)

At Key Stages 1 and 2, only English, mathematics, science and information technology now have to be taught according to the detailed programmes set out in the national curriculum documents. Design and technology, history, geography, music, art and physical education now (from September 1998) have an ambiguous status at these stages. The subjects still have to be taught, but schools no longer have to follow the detailed programmes of study previously in force, and this is to be recognised in OFSTED inspections. A foreign language is not compulsory at these stages. In addition, schools must now devote an hour each day to literacy (from September 1998) and an hour to numeracy (from September 1999) at these stages.

At Key Stage 3, a modern foreign language is added, and all eleven subjects now have to be taught according to the detailed programmes in the national curriculum documents.

At Key Stage 4, history, geography, music and art cease to be compulsory.

The national curriculum in Wales is similar though not identical to that in England. For English, mathematics, science, information technology, design and technology, physical education and modern foreign languages, the programmes of study are the same in both countries (and set out in booklets published jointly by the then Department for Education and the Welsh Office). English, however, is not compulsory at Key Stage 1 in Welsh-speaking schools. For history, geography, music and art, each country has its own programmes of study. In addition, Welsh is a national curriculum subject in Wales: it is currently compulsory at Key Stage 3 in all schools, and also at Key Stage 4 in Welsh-speaking schools, where it is a core subject. From September 1999, it will be compulsory in all Welsh schools at all four Key Stages.

The structure of the national curriculum

The programmes of study for each subject are set out in booklets published in 1995 by the then Department for Education and the Welsh Office (some jointly, some separately). Each subject is divided into different components (or *attainment targets*), as illustrated below for the core subjects of English, mathematics and science.

English	Mathematics	Science
Speaking and listening	Using and applying	Experimental and
Reading	mathematics	investigative science
Writing	Number	Life processes and living
	Algebra (KS 3 and 4)	things
	Shape, space and	Materials and their
	measures	properties
	Handling data (KS 2–4)	Physical processes

For each attainment target in most subjects, nine successive levels of achievement are identified, with *level descriptions* for each, setting out the way pupils should make progress from the beginning of their studies at age five to the end of Key Stage 3 at age 14. These levels do not coincide with Key Stages, as it is recognised that pupils differ in their rates of progress. However, it is specified that by the end of each Key Stage, the great majority of pupils should have levels of attainment within the following ranges.

End of Key Stage 1 – Levels 1–3
End of Key Stage 2 – Levels 2–5
End of Key Stage 3 – Levels 3–7

Level 8 is for 'very able' pupils, and the ninth (unnumbered) level is for 'exceptional performance' at Key Stage 3.

By way of example, here are three of the level descriptions for the reading attainment target in English.

> *Level 1*
>
> Pupils recognise familiar words in simple texts. They use their knowledge of letters and sound–symbol relationships in order to read words and to establish meaning when reading aloud. In these activities they sometimes require support. They express their response to poems, stories and non-fiction by identifying aspects they like.
>
> *Level 5*
>
> Pupils show understanding of a range of texts, selecting essential points and using inference and deduction where appropriate. In their responses, they identify key features, themes and characters, and select sentences, phrases and relevant information to support their views. They retrieve and collate information from a range of sources.
>
> *Exceptional performance*
>
> Pupils confidently sustain their responses to a demanding range of texts, developing their ideas and referring in detail to aspects of language, structure and presentation. They make apt and careful comparison between texts, including consideration of audience, purpose and form. They identify and analyse argument, opinion and alternative interpretations, making cross-references where appropriate.
>
> (DFE/Welsh Office, 1995, pp. 28–9)

These levels of achievement do not apply to Key Stage 4. Nor do they apply to art, music or physical education at any stage: instead, these subjects have *end of key stage descriptions*, setting out the achievements expected of most pupils at the end of each of the four Key Stages.

The national curriculum is not intended to occupy all of pupils' school time, but there are no statutory instructions as to how much time schools should devote to it, or how this time should be divided among the various subjects. However, the Dearing Report, on which the current arrangements for the national curriculum are based (see Chapter 3: 1993 Dearing) makes some recommendations about this, as illustrated in Figure 10.2. (This cannot be compared directly with the pre-1988 Figure 10.1, as the latter gives an *average* of the varied individual curricula actually studied, whereas Figure 10.2 gives recommendations for a suggested *minimum* for *every* child.)

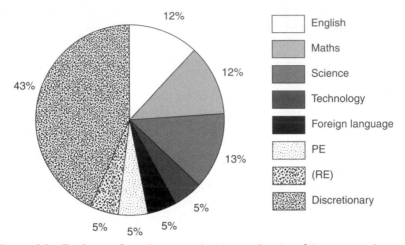

Figure 10.2   The Dearing Report's suggested minimum allocation of time to compulsory subjects at Key Stage 4
(Adapted from Dearing, 1993, Section 5)

In addition, the Government has introduced (from September 1998) a daily 'literacy hour' and (from September 1999) a 'numeracy hour' for primary schools. Though these are not statutory requirements, schools are very strongly encouraged to adopt them, and to follow a detailed schedule of rec-ommended activities in them.

Assessment of the national curriculum

The assessment of pupils' progress through the national curriculum has been greatly simplifed since it was first introduced (see 1987 Black and 1993 Dearing in Chapter 3). Now it is assessed at the end of Key Stages 1, 2 and 3 by a com-bination of assessment by their own teachers and standardised national tests.

In England, at the end of Key Stage 1 (age 7), pupils are assessed by their teachers in the core subjects (English, mathematics, science and information technology) and also take national tests in English and mathematics only. At the end of Key Stage 2 (age 11) pupils are again assessed by their teachers and now take tests in all the core subjects. At the end of Key Stage 3 (age 14) pupils are assessed by their teachers and take national tests in all the subjects (core and foundation) of the national curriculum.

In Wales, Welsh is assessed where appropriate (see above), in place of English at Key Stage 1 and in addition to the other subjects at Key Stages 2 and 3.

At the end of Key Stage 4 (age 16), assessment in both England and Wales is conducted through the GCSE (see Chapter 9).

From September 1998, children are also assessed on entry to primary school (at age 5).

SCOTLAND

The 1988 Education Reform Act does not apply to Scotland, which (uniquely in Europe) does not have a statutory curriculum. However, there is a considerable similarity across the country in what pupils study, for two main reasons.

First, for pupils aged 5–14, the Secretary of State for Scotland and the Scottish Consultative Council on the Curriculum have issued general *guidance* on 'a broad and balanced curriculum', with specific guidance on English, Latin, Gaelic, modern languages, mathematics, environmental studies and religious and moral education.

An important influence on that advice is the Munn Report, which recommended a common curriculum for the third and fourth years of Scottish secondary schools (equivalent to Key Stage 4 in the rest of the United Kingdom). This was a complicated structure of a two-tier core plus an elective area (see Chapter 3: 1977 Munn). The percentages of pupils' time recommended by Munn for the various subjects are shown in Figure 10.3.

Secondly, the education of children over 14 is influenced by the fact that Scotland, unlike England, has only one examination board, and so pupils throughout the country who are taking its Standard or Higher grade examinations (see Chapter 9) follow the same syllabuses (ONS, 1998, Chapter 26).

NORTHERN IRELAND

The 1998 Education Reform Act does not apply to Northern Ireland, which has its own compulsory curriculum for all grant-aided (i.e. maintained) schools. This consists of six areas of study:

- English
- mathematics
- science and technology
- environment and society
- creative and expressive studies
- language studies (secondary schools only)

and six cross-curricular themes:

- cultural heritage
- education for mutual understanding

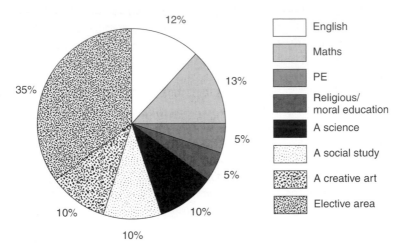

Figure 10.3   The Munn Report's suggested allocation of time to subject areas in the third and fourth years of Scottish secondary education
(Adapted from SED, 1977)

- health education
- information technology
- economic awareness (secondary schools only)
- careers education (secondary schools only

In addition, a religious education syllabus, approved by the four main churches, is also compulsory in grant-aided schools. (Sex education is taught through the science and health education programmes noted above.)

This compulsory curriculum is to occupy 85% of pupils' time in primary and 60–65% in secondary schools.

Compulsory assessment is conducted at the ages of 8 and 11 in English and mathematics, and at the age of 14 in English, mathematics and science. (In schools that use Irish as the medium of instruction, the assessment at age 11 has Irish instead of English, and at ages 11 and 14 has Irish in addition to the other subjects) (ONS, 1998, Chapter 26).

SOURCES AND FURTHER READING

Dearing, R. (1993) *The National Curriculum and its Assessment: Final Report*, London: SCAA.

DES (1987) *Statistical Bulletin 10/87: The Secondary Schooling Staffing Survey – Data on the Curriculum in Maintained Secondary Schools in England*, London: DES.

DFE/Welsh Office (1995) *English in the National Curriculum*, London: HMSO.

DFE/Welsh Office (1995) *Mathematics in the National Curriculum*, London: HMSO.

DFE/Welsh Office (1995) *Science in the National Curriculum*, London: HMSO.

DfEE (1995) *The School Curriculum: a brief guide*, London, DfEE.

ONS (1999) *Britain: the official yearbook of the United Kingdom*, London: The Stationery Office.

SED (1977) *The Structure of the Curriculum in the Third and Fourth Years of the Scottish Secondary School*, Edinburgh: HMSO ('The Munn Report').

As measured by qualifications, educational achievement in the United Kingdom has increased during the last two decades, as Figure 11.1 illustrates. More people now hold qualifications at every level and fewer have no qualifications.

There has also been an increase in recent years in the percentage of young people aged 16–18 staying on in full-time education, as Figure 11.2 shows. Only a minority of these are now in schools – 48% of 16-year-olds, 44% of 17-year-olds and 7% of 18-year-olds. The rest attend institutions of further or higher education.

Educational achievement as measured by participation in higher education has also increased during the past decade, as Figure 11.3 shows.

Different types of school achieve different levels of success in public examinations. Selective schools – whether maintained or independent – predictably have much higher percentages of their pupils achieving top grades than

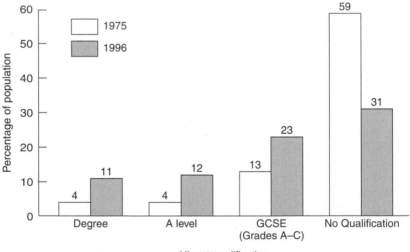

Figure 11.1   *Highest level of qualification held by people aged 16–69 who are not in full-time education, Great Britain 1975 and 1996*
(Adapted from ONS, 1997a, Table 4)
Note: Scottish and older English and Welsh qualifications are treated as equivalent to A level or GCSE as appropriate

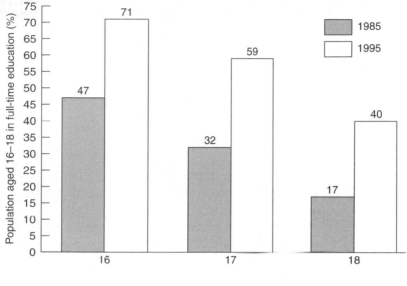

*Figure 11.2   Percentage of population aged 16 18 staying on in full-time education,
England, 1985 and 1995
(Adapted from DfEE, 1996, Tables 7, 9 and 11)*

comprehensive schools. Grant-maintained schools, especially comprehensives, achieve higher figures than their LEA-maintained equivalents.

Education in the United Kingdom is characterised by numerous inequalities in achievement and provision, not only between individuals but also between social groups and categories. The rest of this chapter provides data about three different dimensions of inequality: sex, ethnic group and social class; it also gives some information about educational achievement in independent schools.

SEX

Differences between the sexes in educational participation and achievement are much better documented than any other dimensions of inequality. This is because sex is one of the principal categories used in the collection and publication of official statistics on education. The measures of educational

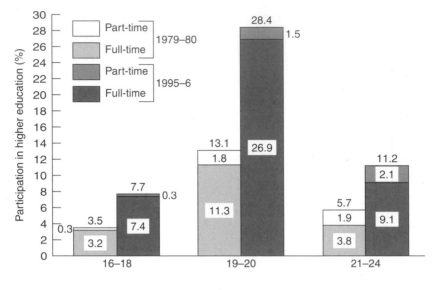

Figure 11.3   Percentage of population in higher education, United Kingdom, 1979–80 and 1995–6
(Adapted from GSS, 1982, Table 29, and 1997, Table 21)

achievement discussed above all show differences between the sexes. Figure 11.4 illustrates how girls do better, overall, than boys in school examinations at all levels.

However, sex differences in achievement are not uniformly in favour of girls across all subjects: while girls regularly achieve higher numbers of passes in some subjects, boys consistently achieve higher numbers in others. Figures 11.5 and 11.6 illustrate this for England, showing the number of 'passes' by boys and by girls in some of the most popular subjects, at GCSE and GCE A level.

By the sixth form, a pattern is well established of arts subjects (especially languages) being predominantly girls' subjects, and maths and sciences (other than biology) being predominantly boys' subjects. Figures 11.7 and 11.8 show how these patterns have been reflected during the past decade, in England, in A-level passes held by school leavers.

Boys are over-represented and girls under-represented in special schools, as compared with their numbers in the population as a whole; this is illustrated in Figure 11.9 using data for England.

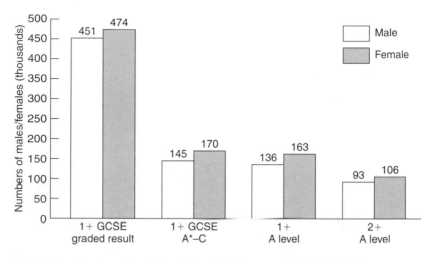

Figure 11.4   Numbers of male/female students of any age in the UK obtaining
GCSE/GCE passes (or the Scottish equivalent), 1995–6
(Adapted from GSS, 1997, Table 29)

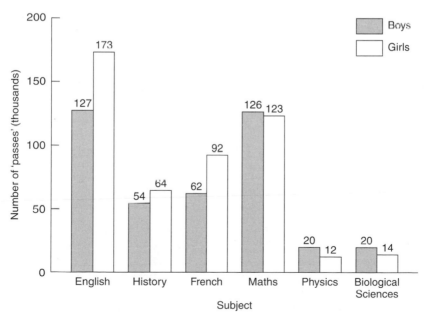

Figure 11.5   GCSE grades A*–C obtained by 15-year-olds by the end of 1995–6, England
(Adapted from DfEE, 1997, Table 9)

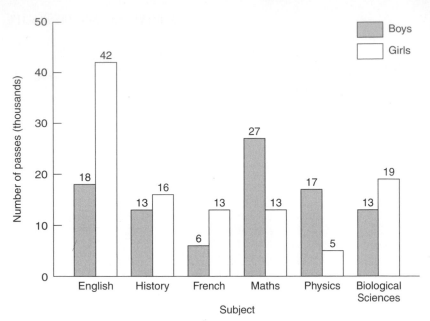

Figure 11.6   A-level passes obtained by 17-year-olds by the end of 1995–6, England
(Adapted from DfEE, 1997, Tables 18 and 19)
Note: AS levels are included, with each AS-level pass counted as half an A-level pass

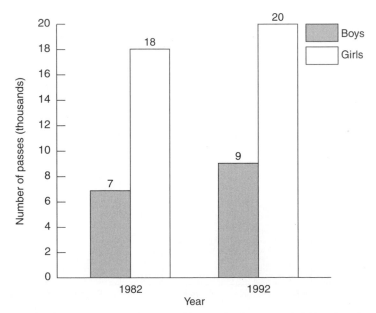

Figure 11.7   A-level passes in French and other modern languages held by school leavers,
England, 1982–92
(Adapted from DES, 1982, Table C13; DFE, 1993, Table 14)

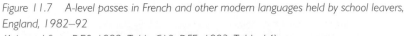

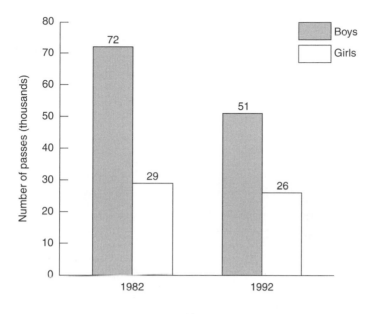

Figure 11.8 A-level passes in maths, physics and chemistry held by school leavers, England, 1982–92
(Adapted from DES, 1982, Table C13; DFE, 1993, Table 14)

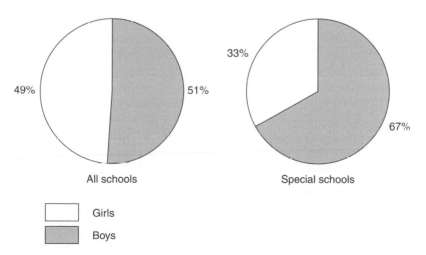

Figure 11.9 Percentages of boys and girls in all maintained schools and in special schools England, 1997
(Adapted from DfEE, 1997, Tables 11 and 31)

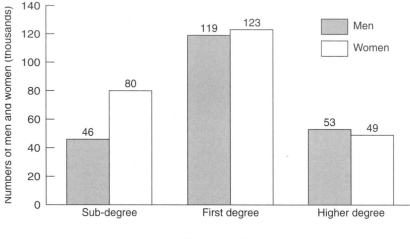

Figure 11.10   Numbers of men and women obtaining different types of higher education
qualification, United Kingdom, 1994–5
(Adapted from GSS, 1997, Table 34)

There are now (1995–6) virtually equal numbers of male and female full-time
students in the UK, but women outnumber men by 55% to 45% among part-
time students (GSS, 1997, Table 22). The numbers of men and women obtaining higher education qualifications of different levels are shown in Figure 11.10.

As with schools, though, these global figures conceal great variation from
subject to subject. Figure 11.11 shows the numbers of first degrees in different
subject areas taken by men and by women in the United Kingdom in the academic year 1994–5. (These figures do not include Open University degrees.)

Differences between the sexes in education patterns are also discussed
below in the section on independent schools. For differences in patterns of
employment in educational institutions, see Chapter 7.

ETHNIC GROUPS

Much less information is available about educational differences and similarities
between ethnic groups than between the sexes, as ethnic divisions are not
categories used in the national collection and publication of official statistics on
education. However, the 1991 Census contained for the first time a question
on ethnic group membership (see Chapter 2), and this provides some informa-

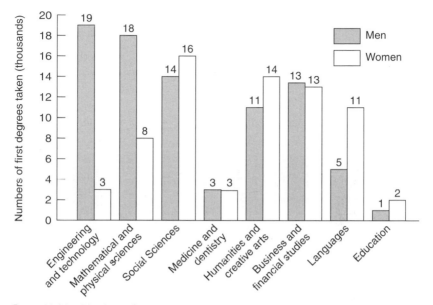

Figure 11.11   Numbers of men and women taking first degrees in selected subjects (other than Open University), United Kingdom, 1994–5 (Adapted from GSS, 1997, Table 34)

tion about differences between the groups in educational attainment, as Figure 11.12 illustrates. In interpreting these figures, however, it must be borne in mind that there may be other differences between the characteristics of 'ethnic groups' as well as ethnicity. For example, different ethnic groups are often of very different social class composition (see Chapter 2, Figure 2.13).

Among current students in higher education, ethnic minorities are more highly represented than the white population. For example, 12.2% of 18–20-year-old students in higher education belong to minority ethnic groups, compared with 7.3% of the 18–20-year-old population as a whole. But the picture of ethnic minority participation is varied here too.

● There are large variations among different minority ethnic groups. In particular, Afro-Caribbean men and Bangladeshi women are under-represented in higher education.

● There are large differences between different types of university, with Black students concentrated in the former polytechnics and colleges of higher education that became universities after 1992 (see Chapter 5). Just under three-quarters of all Black students attend these universities, compared with just under half of white and of Asian students (Coffield and Vignoles, 1997).

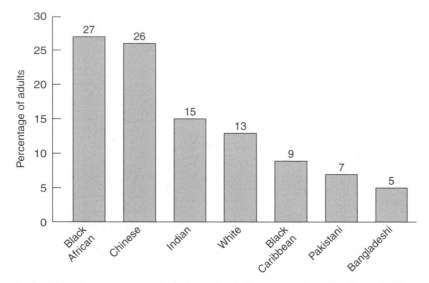

Figure 11.12   Percentage of adults in the main ethnic groups of the 1991 Census holding qualifications higher than A level
(Adapted from OPCS/General Register Office for Scotland, 1993, Vol. 2, Table 17)

For differences between ethnic groups in patterns of employment in schools, see Chapter 7.

SOCIAL CLASS

Although social class is one of the census categories (see Chapter 2), it is not widely used in the publication of official statistics on education. Nor have there been many recent sample-survey investigations of the relationship between social class and educational attainment. One reason for this relative neglect may be that so many earlier surveys gave such clear and unequivocal results: at virtually every stage of education, by virtually every criterion of achievement, middle-class children had higher levels of achievement than working-class children. This was documented particularly thoroughly in surveys conducted for a succession of official reports in the 1950s and 1960s (see Chapter 3, especially 1954 Gurney-Dixon, 1959 Crowther, 1963 Newsom, 1963–4 Robbins and 1967 Plowden), whose criteria of educational achievement ranged from 11 plus passes to class of university degree.

In the 1950s and 1960s, most of those surveyed were, or had been, at school under the tripartite system. There has been little research in most of the United Kingdom into the relative effects of social class on achievement under the tripartite and comprehensive systems. In Scotland, however, while differences between the social classes in educational attainment remain, they are smaller in the com-

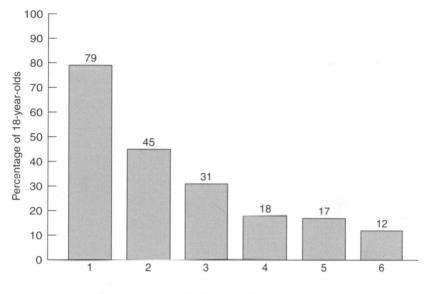

Figure 11.13   Percentages of 18-year-olds from each socioeconomic group who participated in higher education, Great Britain, 1995–6
(Adapted from Robertson and Vignoles, 1997, Table 1.2)
Key to socioeconomic groups: 1 Professional; 2 Employers and managers; 3 Intermediate and junior non-manual; 4 Skilled manual and self-employed non-professional; 5 Semi-skilled manual and personal service; 6 Unskilled manual

prehensive system than they were in the tripartite. The trend towards equality of attainment is especially marked in schools that have been comprehensive for a long time. It has been a result of the raising of working-class attainment, not the lowering of middle-class attainment (McPherson and Willms, 1987).

At higher education level, the link between social class and educational achievement remains strong, as Figure 11.13 illustrates.

However, these figures represent a slight diminution of class differences in recent years, as the expansion of higher education has benefited the 'lower' groups more than the 'higher'. At the extremes, the participation rate of 18-year-olds from the unskilled manual socioeconomic group doubled between 1991–2 and 1995–6 (from 6% to 12%), compared with a rise of less than half for the professional group (from 55% to 79%).

The number of people with fathers in the professional group is relatively small, so that they are still a minority of those who have been to university: see Figure 11.14.

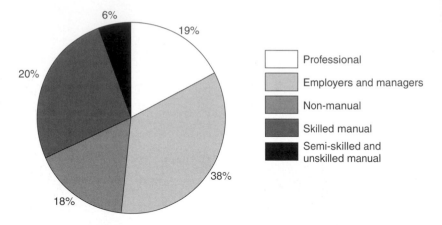

*Figure 11.14   Socioeconomic groups of fathers of people whose last full-time education
was at university, Great Britain, 1991–2
(Adapted from OPCS, 1993, Table 10.4b)*

People's own occupational levels are also strongly related to their levels of
educational attainment. This is illustrated in Figure 11.15, which shows the percentages of people in each socioeconomic group with various levels of educational qualification.

INDEPENDENT SCHOOLS

Pupils in independent schools (see Chapter 5) form a small percentage of all
school pupils – just over 7% in the United Kingdom in 1991–2. However, independent schools retain a much higher proportion of their pupils after the legal
minimum school-leaving age than do maintained schools, so that in 1991–2,
18% of all boys and 15% of all girls aged 16 or over were in independent
schools. This shows a percentage decline since 1951 (when the corresponding
figure for boys was 29%, or 38% including direct grant schools); during this
period, there was a substantial increase in *absolute* numbers over the minimum
leaving age in independent schools, but this was overshadowed by a much
larger increase, proportionately as well as absolutely, in maintained schools.
(Figures for 1951 have been taken, and rounded, from Halsey, Heath and
Ridge, 1984, Table 1; 1991–2 figures from CSO, 1994, Table 3.7; GSS, 1994,
Table 15).

The percentage of pupils in independent schools is significantly higher in
England (8%) than in Scotland (3%), Wales (3%), or Northern Ireland (1%).

Fees for independent schools are high. For example, the average annual fees

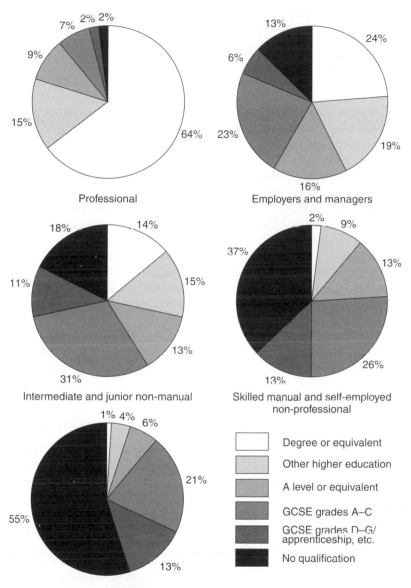

Figure 11.15   *Highest qualification shown as percentage of each socioeconomic group,*
Great Britain, 1994 and 1995 combined
(Adapted from ONS, 1997a, Table 3)
Note: The figures for 'intermediate and junior non-manual' and for 'semi-skilled and
unskilled manual' each combine two OPCS categories; people with qualifications other than
those above (e.g. from abroad) are omitted; the sample is confined to economically active
people aged 25–60 not in full-time education

in Headmasters' Conference Schools in 1999 were £13,500 for boarders, and £5,700 for day pupils. In schools belonging to the Girls' Schools Association, the average annual fees were £12,700 for boarders, and £5,500 for day pupils (ISIS, 1999).

Approximately 33,000 pupils, 7% of pupils in independent schools in the UK, hold places under the Assisted Places Scheme, which provides assistance with tuition fees and certain other expenses. A further 95,000 in schools belonging to ISIS (20%) receive help with fees from the schools themselves, 3,000 (1%) from local authorities and 12,000 (3%) from other sources (ISIS, 1999, Table 7). (However, the Assisted Places Scheme is currently being phased out.)

Independent schools draw their pupils unequally from the different social classes, but there have been no recent attempts to quantify these differences. The last large-scale study to do so covered men who had completed their formal education by 1972: it found that 27% of men with fathers in professional or managerial occupations went to independent schools, compared to 7% of the sons of routine, non-manual workers and small proprietors, and 1% of the sons of manual workers (Halsey, Heath and Ridge, 1980, 1984).

Pupils in independent schools achieve levels of success in public examinations higher than those at maintained comprehensive schools, but lower than those at maintained selective schools. For example, 87% of 15-year-olds at independent schools obtain five or more GCSE 'passes' (i.e. Grades A*–C), compared with 44% of those at maintained comprehensive schools and 95% of those at maintained selective schools (1996–7 figures: DfEE 1998, Table 3a).

Attitudes to private schools are summarised in Figure 11.16, which shows the percentages of people in Great Britain (in 1987) who thought there should be more, fewer, none, or about the same number as then.

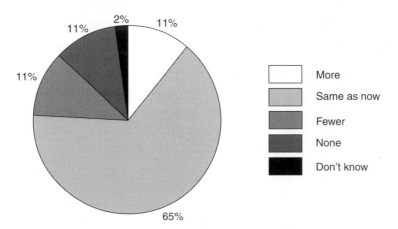

Figure 11.16   Attitudes to private schools, Great Britain, 1987
(Adapted from Flather, 1988, p. 22)

There is little variation with age or sex in these attitudes, but some variation between social classes. Respondents in non-manual occupations are more likely to think that there should be more private schools, or the same number as now, than respondents in manual occupations (77% compared with 62%).

SOURCES AND FURTHER READING

Coffield, F. and Vignoles, A. (1997) *Widening Participation in Higher Education by Ethnic Minorities, Women and Alternative Students, Report 5 of the National Committee of Inquiry into Higher Education*, London: DfEE.

CSO (1994) *Social Trends*, No. 24, 1994 edn., London: HMSO.

DES (1982) *Statistics of Education 1982: School Leavers CSE and GCE*, London: HMSO.

DFE (1993) *Statistics of Education: Public Examinations: GCSE and GCE, 1992*, London: HMSO.

DfEE (1996) *News DfEE 213/96: Participation in education and training by 16–18 year-olds in England: 1985–1995*, London: DfEE.

DfEE (1997) *Statistics of Education: Public Examinations: GCSE and GCE in England 1996*, London: The Stationery Office.

Flather, P. (1988) Education matters, in Jowell, R., Witherspoon, S. and Brooks, L. (eds) *British Social Attitudes: The 1986 Report*, Aldershot: Gower.

GSS (1982) *Educational Statistics for the United Kingdom 1982*, London: HMSO.

GSS (1994) *Educational Statistics for the United Kingdom 1993*, London: HMSO.

GSS (1997) *Educational Statistics for the United Kingdom*, London: The Stationery Office.

Halsey, A. H., Heath, A. F. and Ridge, J. M. (1980) *Origins and Destinations: Family, Class and Education in Modern Britain*, Oxford: Clarendon Press.

Halsey, A. H., Heath, A. F. and Ridge, J. M. (1984) 'The political arithmetic of public schools' in Walford, G. (ed.) *British Public Schools: Policy and Practice*, pp. 9–44, London: Falmer Press.

ISIS (1999) *ISIS Annual Census 1999*, London: ISIS.

McPherson, A. F. and Willms, J. D. (1987) Equalisation and improvement: some effects of comprehensive reorganisation in Scotland, *Sociology*, Vol. 21, No. 4.

ONS (1997a) *Living in Britain: results from the 1995 General Household Survey*, London: The Stationery Office.

ONS (1997b) *Regional Trends 32: 1997 edn*, London: The Stationery Office.

OPCS (1993) *General Household Survey 1991*, No. 22, London: HMSO.

OPCS/General Register Office for Scotland (1993) *1991 Census: Ethnic Group and Country of Birth: Great Britain*, London: HMSO.

Robertson, D. and Vignoles, A. (1997) *Widening Participation in Higher Education for Students from Lower Socioeconomic Groups and Students with Disabilities*, Report 6 of the National Committee of Inquiry into Higher Education, London: DfEE.

Vocational and pre-vocational training programmes, aimed primarily at school leavers and long-term unemployed adults, are similar in the different countries of the United Kingdom, but they are organised and administered separately. In this chapter, we first describe the English arrangements in some detail, then note the principal similarities and differences in Wales, Northern Ireland and Scotland.

ENGLAND

In England until 1995, 'education' and vocational 'training' were the responsibility of separate government departments, but the creation then of the Department for Education and Employment (DfEE) has brought them closer together. Shortly thereafter, the bodies responsible for school curriculum and assessment and for vocational qualifications were also merged, to form the Qualifications and Curriculum Authority (QCA).

The percentage of young people staying on in full-time education after the legal minimum leaving age has increased substantially in recent years, as has the likelihood that their post-compulsory education will be in further (or higher) education rather than school. This is shown, for 16-, 17- and 18-year-olds, in Figure 12.1.

During the 1990s, there has been an increase in the unemployment rates of young people (aged 16–19). Between 1991 and 1997, the unemployment rate for young men rose from 16.4% to 18.2% of all the economically active. For young women, the rates also rose, from 12.7% to 14.0% (ONS, 1998, Table 4.25).

VOCATIONAL TRAINING SCHEMES

In addition to employment and conventional education in schools or colleges, young people, especially school leavers aged 16 and 17, have a number of vocational and pre-vocational training schemes available to them. Some of these schemes operate within or partly within schools and colleges, others outside. They are under the auspices of the Department for Education and Employment (DfEE), though it does not itself organise training programmes and courses, but instead delegates the tasks to Training and Enterprise Councils (TECs) throughout the country (with responsibilities for supporting new businesses, as well as for training). TECs are independent, non-profit-making companies, with boards of directors led by business people from the private sector. There are currently 75 TECs in England. The DfEE enters into contracts with each of

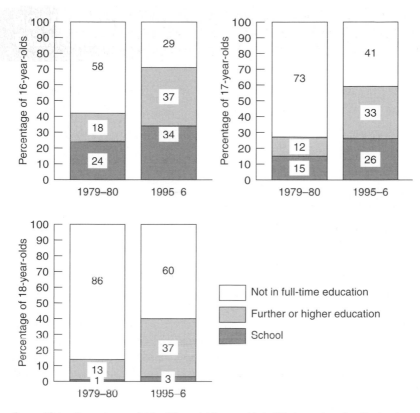

*Figure 12.1   Percentages of 16-, 17- and 18-year-olds in full-time education, England,
1979–80 and 1995–6
(Adapted from DFE, 1993 and DfEE, 1996, Tables 7, 9 and 11)*

these for managing the local provision of training for young people and unemployed adults, and fostering links more generally between business and education. The TECs in their turn entered into contracts with local providers of
training, such as colleges and employers.

The main training schemes under the auspices of the DfEE are described
below. There are numerous other, smaller schemes, but these four between
them account for most of the expenditure of the DfEE on training and enterprise.

Work-Based Training for Adults

The Training for Work programme began in April 1993, with the aim of
helping long-term unemployed people – especially those who had been

unemployed for over 12 months – to improve their skills and find jobs. It was designed to be flexible, allowing the TECs who ran it to offer the types of training and combinations of training and work experience that they judged appropriate for individual needs and local labour market conditions. An estimated 200,000 people enrolled on TfW programmes in 1997–8, with a total expenditure of £424 million. Of these, an estimated 30% obtained NVQs, and 46% found jobs (DfEE/OFSTED, 1998, Table 3.20).

TfW replaced various earlier training programmes for unemployed adults, aged 18–63, and is itself being replaced from 1998–9 by *Work-Based Training for Adults*.

Work-Based Training for Young People

There are now two main training schemes for young people, under the auspices of the DfEE and run by TECs: *National Traineeships* and *Modern Apprenticeships*.

National Traineeships introduced at the end of 1997 in 25 employment sectors, expanded substantially in 1998–9. Successful trainees will obtain qualifications at NVQ Level 2 (see Chapter 9).

Modern Apprenticeships were introduced on a national scale from 1995. Their aim was to build on the best of traditional apprenticeships in sectors which had used them, and to introduce apprenticeships to other sectors. The apprentice, his or her employer and the responsible TEC are required to sign an 'apprenticeship pledge', describing the training to be provided, and committing all parties to seeing it through.

Successful trainees will obtain qualifications at NVQ Level 3 (see chapter 9).

Estimated spending for 1997–8 on both these and other, smaller schemes is £731 million. An estimated 209,000 young people enrolled on the schemes, and 65,000 will obtain an NVQ (including NVQ Level 2 obtained on Modern Apprenticeships en route to Level 3) (DfEE/OFSTED, 1998, Table 2.14).

WALES

Training in Wales is the responsibility of the Welsh Office. Although the Welsh arrangements are separate from those in England, they are very similar. Thus Wales also has Work-Based Training for Adults, National Traineeships and Modern Apprenticeships, aimed at NVQs and organised by its three TECs. In 1997–8, an estimated 8,400 adults began training; 52% of those leaving training courses obtained jobs, and 35% of those leaving obtained at least one NVQ at Level 1. At the same time, an estimated 22,000 young people were on training courses, and 60% of leavers obtained at least one NVQ at Level 1 (Welsh Office/OHMCI, 1998, Tables 4.09 and 4.10).

SCOTLAND

Training in Scotland is the responsibility of the Scottish Office Education and Industry Department, much of it organised and financed through the Scottish Enterprise and the Highlands and Islands Enterprise programmes. Like England and Wales, Scotland operates work-based training programmes for adults and for young people. Much of the training is delivered through 22 Local Enterprise Companies (LECs), the Scottish counterpart to Training and Enterprise Councils, though with slightly different responsibilities. (LECs, for example, have some responsibilities for environmental protection.)

In 1996–7, 38,500 school leavers began training, and 37% of those leaving gained recognised qualifications. (In these figures, Scottish Enterprise and Highlands and Islands Enterprise programmes are taken together.)

In 1996–7, 29,300 adults began training, and 36% of those leaving gained recognised qualifications or found jobs. (In these figures, Scottish Enterprise and Highlands and Islands Enterprise programmes are again taken together) (Departments of the Secretary of State for Scotland etc, 1998, Chapter 4).

NORTHERN IRELAND

Training in Northern Ireland is the responsibility of the Training and Employment Agency of the Northern Ireland Office Department of Economic Development. The Agency has a staff of 1,160, and had a 1997–8 budget of £196 million. The main training and employment schemes under its auspices are described below (Northern Ireland Office Department of Finance and Personnel/HM Treasury, 1998, Chapter 6).

Jobskills Programme

Unlike the rest of the UK, which has separate training schemes for young people and adults, Northern Ireland has a single programme for everyone over 16. Programmes last up to three years, and are aimed at NVQ Level 2 (see Chapter 9). It was introduced in 1995, and is organised through a network of approved training organisations. In 1997–8 (the end of its first full three-year cycle), it had a total expenditure of £71 million. It had 15,000 trainees at a time, on average, of whom 55% obtained at least one NVQ at Level 2.

Action for Community Employment (ACE)

The Action for Community Employment programme provides temporary employment – up to one year – for long-term unemployed adults, on projects deemed to be of benefit to the community; most of the projects are run by voluntary organisations. The programme has an element of structured training.

The average number of places on ACE at any one time in 1997–8 was an estimated 5,200. The estimated expenditure on the ACE for 1997–8 was £29 million. (The programme is being contracted as the economy grows and unemployment falls.)

SOURCES AND FURTHER READING

Departments of the Secretary of State for Scotland and the Forestry Commission (1998) *Serving Scotland's Needs: The Government's Expenditure Plans 1998–99*, Cm 3914, Edinburgh: The Stationery Office.

DFE (1993) *Statistical Bulletin 16/93: Participation in Education by 16–18-year-olds in England: 1979/93*, London: DFE.

DfEE (1996) NEWS DfEE 213/96: *Participation in education and training by 16–18 year olds in England: 1985 to 1995*, London: DfEE.

DfEE and OFSTED (1998) *Departmental Report: The Government's Expenditure Plans 1998–99*, Cm 3610, London: The Stationery Office.

Northern Ireland Office Department of Finance and Personnel/HM Treasury (1998) *Northern Ireland Expenditure Plans and Priorities: The Government's Expenditure Plans 1998–99*, Cm 3916, London: The Stationery Office.

ONS (1998) *Social Trends 28*, London: The Stationery Office.

OPCS (1994) *General Household Survey 1992*, London: HMSO.

Welsh Office/OHMCI (1998) *The Government's Expenditure Plans 1998–99: Departmental Report by the Welsh Office and the Office of Her Majesty's Chief Inspector of Schools in Wales*, Cm 3915, London: The Stationery Office.

Aided School type of voluntary school where the voluntary body retains control over the employment of teachers, religious instruction and admissions policy, in exchange for meeting part of the external maintenance costs

Ancillary Staff non-teaching staff in schools (e.g. laboratory assistants, caretakers, secretaries) and unqualified classroom assistants

Assisted Places Scheme a scheme introduced in the 1980 Education Act whereby central government pays part of the tuition costs (on a means-tested basis) for children who have been in state schools to attend selected independent day schools (now being disbanded)

Banding modified form of streaming, where pupils are divided into broad bands of ability (e.g. average, below average, above average) and each band follows a similar curriculum

Capping mechanism by which central government sets limits to the amount of money a local authority is allowed to raise through the Council Tax

Catchment Area the area from which a school takes its pupils

City Technology College school with a technological bias, set up by private sponsors with government grants

Community Home replaced approved schools under the 1969 Children and Young Persons Act. Administered by Social Services Departments

Comprehensive School secondary school which does not select children for admission on the grounds of ability

Consortium

group of schools which join together for a particular purpose, for example to purchase equipment or to teach certain subjects (especially at sixth-form level, where falling rolls would otherwise result in sixth-form groups being too small)

Continuous Assessment

judging students on the basis of work done during a course rather than, or in addition to, a formal examination at the end

Controlled School

in Great Britain a type of voluntary school where all costs are met by the LEA but the voluntary body retains some rights over religious instruction. In Northern Ireland, a school financed and managed by an Education and Library Board

'Crammer'

private institution providing intensive coaching for examinations

Curriculum

course of study followed by a pupil or student

Developmental Curriculum

a type of curriculum deemed suitable for children with severe learning difficulties. It has closely defined educational and social objectives, and aims to encourage a degree of personal autonomy (see also Mainstream plus Support Curriculum; Modified Curriculum)

Dyslexia

disability in using and interpreting written language and symbols, irrespective of general intelligence and spoken language skills. (Its existence is widely, but not universally, accepted by educational psychologists.)

Education Authority

the Scottish term for a local education authority. As in England and Wales, EAs form part of the local government structure

Education and Library Board

in Northern Ireland, one of the five regional educational authorities, centrally appointed by the Department of Education Northern Ireland, though partly consisting of local council representatives. It is funded by the DENI. It has complete responsibility for controlled schools and for some services to all schools in its geographical area

Education Otherwise

an organisation offering support and help to parents wishing to educate their children out of school (the name is based on a phrase in the 1944 Education Act)

Education Support Grant

sum of money earmarked in the Government's Revenue Support Grant for specific projects which the Secretary of State has decided are important, e.g. science teaching in primary schools. LEAs then bid for this money

First School

primary school taking children from age five up to the age of transfer to middle school at eight or nine

Governor

elected, co-opted, appointed or foundation member of the governing body which every maintained school is now required to have

Grammar School

in the tripartite system in England and Wales, a secondary school taking only children of high academic ability, usually measured by a test taken at age 11 (the tripartite system is now largely replaced, in Great Britain, by comprehensive schools)

Integration

the education of children with special educational needs alongside their peers in ordinary, rather than special, schools. The term is also used in Northern Ireland to refer to education without denominational segregation

Intermediate Treatment	a form of provision dating from the Children and Young Persons Act (1969) for children deemed to be at risk and in trouble, which often includes persistent truants and pupils whom schools are unable to contain. Run by social services, but LEAs may provide teachers
Junior Secondary School	the Scottish equivalent of the secondary modern school in England and Wales
Local Education Authority	in England and Wales, part of the local government structure, responsible for the day-to-day running of the state education service in a particular geographical area (for Northern Ireland, see Education and Library Board)
Mainstream	an ordinary, rather than a special, school, class, etc. (in America, the term 'mainstreaming' is the equivalent of 'integration')
Mainstream plus Support Curriculum	a type of curriculum deemed suitable for children with particular kinds of special need. As the name suggests, this is comparable to ordinary curricula in aims, content and standards, but with support appropriate for pupils' distinctive needs – whether in organisation, equipment or style of teaching (see also Modified Curriculum; Developmental Curriculum)
Maintained School	in Great Britain, a school maintained by the state (see also Voluntary Schools). In Northern Ireland, a school provided by the Roman Catholic Church, though with a large measure of state support and controlled by the Maintained Schools Commission (similar to an aided school in Great Britain)

Middle School	comprehensive school catering for children aged from eight to nine to 12 or 13. Legally designated as either primary or secondary depending on whether most children are under or over age 11. Confined almost entirely to England
Modified Curriculum	a type of curriculum deemed suitable for children with moderate learning difficulties. Similar to ordinary school curricula, but with objectives suited to the children's special needs (see also Mainstream plus Support Curriculum; Developmental Curriculum)
National Curriculum	a set of subjects which the government decides all children must study, with their performance assessed against set criteria at various ages. Applies to England and Wales but not to Scotland or Northern Ireland
Northern Ireland Curriculum	the Northern Ireland equivalent of the English and Welsh National Curriculum
Peripatetic Teacher	visiting teacher, i.e. one who is not attached to any one school but travels to several (e.g. to teach music or to give specialist help for deaf children)
Preparatory School	private, fee-charging school for children between the ages of eight and 11 (girls) or 13 (boys), preparing them for entrance examinations for the independent secondary and public schools
Public School	usually used, especially in England, to refer to one of the prestigious independent schools for boys. In Scotland, however, 'public school' refers to a maintained school

Pupil Profile
form of evaluation designed to give more detailed information about a pupil than an examination result. It may include academic grades, but also such things as internal school assessments, material selected by the pupil and teachers' comments

Quality Assurance Agency
established in 1997, the Agency conducts quality audits and assessments of higher education institutions on behalf of the Higher Education Funding Council for England, and advises the Government as to whether HE establishments should be empowered to award degrees, or given university status

Reception Class
the first class of an infant or first school, taking children at (or before) the age of five

Revenue Support Grant
money allocated to local authorities by the government to supplement the local Council Tax. Each authority decides what proportion to spend on education

Rising Fives
children who are not yet five years old, admitted to schools in the term before their fifth birthday, or in some areas at the beginning of the school year in which they will become five

Sandwich Course
course with periods of study at a university or college, alternating with periods of training and experience in industry, commerce or the professions

Secondary Intermediate School
the Northern Ireland equivalent of the secondary modern school in England and Wales (often referred to simply as a 'secondary' school)

Secondary Modern School
in the tripartite system in England and Wales, a secondary school which caters for those children, identified as of average and below average academic ability, who do not

go to grammar schools. (The tripartite system is now replaced in most of Great Britain, by comprehensive schools.)

Senior Secondary School   the Scottish equivalent of the grammar school in England and Wales

Setting   grouping pupils according to ability in a particular subject. A student may thus be in one set for English, another for mathematics, etc.

Sixth Form College   separate college for 16–19-year-olds, taking pupils from several schools in an area

Special Agreement School   type of secondary school with rights and responsibilities similar to those of an aided school. Set up by a special agreement for joint provision made between a voluntary body and an LEA before the 1944 Education Act

Special Educational Needs   term introduced by the Warnock Report to replace the old categories of handicap

Special School   separate school for children with learning, physical or emotional difficulties

Statement   formal document drawn up by an LEA (in consultation with parents) describing the special educational needs of a child who needs more help than can be provided within the ordinary resources of a school. The assessment procedure leading to a statement was first laid down in the 1981 Education Act

Streaming   allocating pupils, on the basis of perceived ability, to 'streams', i.e. classes in which pupils stay for all subjects, usually following different curricula

Supply Teacher   teacher appointed by an LEA or GM school to fill in for absent school staff, for periods ranging from half a day to several weeks

Teacher Placement Service government-funded scheme operating in England, Wales and Scotland to support short-term teacher placements in industry, business and the public sector

Tertiary College college for young people over the age of 16 that combines the functions of a sixth form and FE college by offering a full range of academic and vocational courses

Twenty-one-hour Rule rule enabling claimants of Unemployment or Supplementary Benefit to take part-time further education courses, provided that these do not exceed 21 hours a week, and the claimant remains 'available for work'

Upper School comprehensive school taking children after they have left a middle school at 12 or 13. (Some secondary schools also use the term to describe the senior half of the school, as opposed to the 'lower school' comprising the first, second and third years.)

Urban Programme administered by the Department of the Environment. Some grants are given for educational purposes, e.g. setting up nurseries in deprived areas

Vocational Education employment-related rather than academic education

Voluntary School school provided by a voluntary body (usually the church) but maintained by the LEA in England and Wales, and partly aided by the DENI in Northern Ireland (see Aided, Controlled and Special Agreement Schools)

The use of acronyms and abbreviations is extremely widespread in writings about education; this chapter contains only a highly selective list of some of the most common and most important. Some obsolete acronyms are included (and noted as obsolete), since they are still to be found in recent publications.

ACAC   Awdurdod Cwricwlwm ac Asesu Cymru (Curriculum and Assessment Authority for Wales) (now replaced: see ACCAC)

ACCAC   Awdurdod Cymwysterau, Cwricwlwm ac Asesu Cymru (Qualifications, Curriculum and Assessment Authority for Wales)

ACE   Advisory Centre for Education or Action for Community Employment (Northern Ireland)

AEB   Associated Examining Board

AMA   Association of Metropolitan Authorities

APS   Assisted Places Scheme (now being disbanded)

AS   Advanced Supplementary (examination) (to be renamed Advanced Subsidiary)

AT   Attainment Target

ATL   Association of Teachers and Lecturers

AUT   Association of University Teachers

BA   Bachelor of Arts

BACIFHE British Accreditation Council for Independent Further and Higher Education

BD   Bachelor of Divinity

BEd   Bachelor of Education

BERA   British Educational Research Association

BLitt   Bachelor of Letters

BPhil   Bachelor of Philosophy

BPS   British Psychological Society

BSc   Bachelor of Science

BSL   British Sign Language

BTEC   Business and Technology Education Council (now Edexcel)

CACE   Central Advisory Council for Education (now disbanded)

CAL   Computer Assisted Learning

CASE   Campaign for the Advancement of State Education

CAT   Credit Accumulation and Transfer

CCEA   Council for the Curriculum, Examinations and Assessment (Northern Ireland)

CDT	Craft, Design and Technology (now replaced by Design and Technology in the National Curriculum)
CE2L	Centre for Teaching English as a Second Language
CEO	Chief Education Officer
CET	Continuing Education and Training
CGLI	City and Guilds of London Institute
CIPFA	Chartered Institute of Public Finance and Accountancy
CNAA	Council for National Academic Awards (dissolved in 1992)
COPE	Committee on Primary Education (Scotland)
COSE	Committee on Secondary Education (Scotland)
CPD	Continuing Professional Development
CQSW	Certificate of Qualification in Social Work
CRAC	Careers Research and Advisory Centre
CRE	Commission for Racial Equality
CSO	Central Statistical Office (replaced by ONS)
CSYS	Certificate of Sixth Year Studies (Scotland)
CTC	City Technology College
CVCP	Committee of Vice Chancellors and Principals of the Universities of the United Kingdom
DD	Doctor of Divinity
DENI	Department of Education Northern Ireland
DES	Department of Education and Science (now renamed: see DfEE)
DFE	Department for Education (now renamed: see DfEE)
DfEE	Department for Education and Employment
DipHE	Diploma in Higher Education
DLitt	Doctor of Letters
DPhil	Doctor of Philosophy
DSc	Doctor of Science
DSS	Department of Social Security
EA	Education Authority (Scotland)
EAZ	Education Action Zone
EBP	Education–Business Partnership
ECCTIS	Educational Counselling and Credit Transfer Information Service
ED	Employment Department (now disbanded)
EDG	Employment Department Group (now disbanded)
EFL	English as a Foreign Language
EHE	Enterprise in Higher Education
EIS	Educational Institute of Scotland
EOC	Equal Opportunities Commission
ERA	Education Reform Act (of 1988)
ERIC	Educational Resources Information Centre

ESG	Education Support Grant
ESL	English as a Second Language
ESN	Educationally Subnormal. ESN (M) = moderate. ESN (S) = severe. (no longer used)
EWO	Education Welfare Officer
FAS	Funding Agency for Schools (now disbanded)
FE	Further Education
FEFC	Further Education Funding Council
FEFCW	Further Education Funding Council for Wales
FTE	Full-time Equivalent
GAMMA	Girls and Mathematics Association
GBA	Governing Bodies Association (of boys' public schools)
GBGSA	Governing Bodies of Girls' Schools Association
GCE	General Certificate of Education
GCSE	General Certificate of Secondary Education
GEST	Grants for Education Support and Training
GIST	Girls into Science and Technology
GM	Grant-Maintained
GNVQ	General National Vocational Qualification
GPDST	Girls' Public Day School Trust
GRO	Government Regional Office
GSA	Girls' Schools Association
GSVQ	General Scottish Vocational Qualification
GTC	General Teaching Council
HE	Higher Education
HEFCE	Higher Education Funding Council for England
HEFCS	Higher Education Funding Council for Scotland
HEFCW	Higher Education Funding Council for Wales
HEI	Higher Education Institution
HMC	Headmasters' Conference
HMCI	Her Majesty's Chief Inspector of Schools
HMI	Her Majesty's Inspector (or Inspectorate)
HMSO	Her Majesty's Stationery Office (now The Stationery Office Ltd)
HNC	Higher National Certificate
HND	Higher National Diploma
IAPS	Incorporated Association of Preparatory Schools
IB	International Baccalaureate
ICT	Information and Communication Technology
ILA	Individual Learning Account
ILEA	Inner London Education Authority (now abolished)
INSET	In-service Education of Teachers
IQ	Intelligence Quotient

ISA	Independent Schools Association
ISC	Independent Schools Council
ISIS	Independent Schools Information Service
IT	Information Technology
	or
	Intermediate Treatment
ITT	Initial Teacher Training
JBPVE	Joint Board for Pre-vocational Education
JSA	Job Seekers' Allowance
KS	Key Stage
LCCI	London Chamber of Commerce and Industry
LEA	Local Education Authority
LEC	Local Enterprise Company (Scotland)
LLB	Bachelor of Laws
LLD	Doctor of Laws
LMS	Local Management of Schools
MA	Master of Arts
MBA	Master of Business Administration
MEd	Master of Education
MLD	Moderate Learning Difficulties
MLitt	Master of Letters
MPhil	Master of Philosophy
MSc	Master of Science
NAHT	National Association of Head Teachers
NAME	National Antiracist Movement in Education (formerly National Association for Multiracial Education)
NASUWT	National Association of Schoolmasters Union of Women Teachers
NATE	National Association for the Teaching of English
NATFHE	National Association of Teachers in Further and Higher Education
NCB	National Children's Bureau
NCDS	National Child Development Study
NCET	National Council for Educational Technology
NCVQ	National Council for Vocational Qualifications (now replaced by QCA)
NEC	National Extension College
NFER	National Foundation for Educational Research
NICED	Northern Ireland Council for Educational Development
NICER	Northern Ireland Council for Educational Research
NNEB	National Nursery Examination Board
NUS	National Union of Students
NUSS	National Union of School Students

NUT	National Union of Teachers
NVQ	National Vocational Qualification
OECD	Organisation for Economic Cooperation and Development
OFSTED	Office for Standards in Education
OHMCI	Office of Her Majesty's Chief Inspector of Schools (in practice, usually used only in Wales; the English OHMCI is usually known as OFSTED)
ONC	Ordinary National Certificate
OND	Ordinary National Diploma
OU	Open University
PAT	Professional Association of Teachers
PGCE	Postgraduate Certificate in Education
PhD	Doctor of Philosophy
PoS	Programme of Study
PSLA	Pre-School Learning Alliance
PTA	Parent–Teacher Association
PTR	Pupil/Teacher Ratio
PVC	Pro Vice Chancellor
QAA	Quality Assurance Agency (for higher education)
QCA	Qualifications and Curriculum Authority
QTS	Qualified Teacher Status
RAE	Research Assessment Exercise
REB	Regional Examining Body
RSA	Royal Society of Arts
RSG	Revenue Support Grant
SAAS	Student Awards Agency for Scotland
SAT	Standard Assessment Task
SCAA	School Curriculum and Assessment Authority (now replaced by QCA)
SCCC	Scottish Consultative Council on the Curriculum
SCE	Scottish Certificate of Education
SCET	Scottish Council for Educational Technology
SCITT	School Centred Initial Teacher Training
SCOTCATS	Scottish Credit Accumulation and Transfer Scheme
SCOTVEC	Scottish Vocational Education Council (now replaced by SQA)
SEB	Scottish Examination Board (now replaced by SQA)
SED	Scottish Education Department (renamed: see SOEID)
SEN	Special Educational Needs
SEO	Society of Education Officers
SHA	Secondary Heads Association
SHEFC	Scottish Higher Education Funding Council
SHMIS	Society of Headmasters and Headmistresses of Independent Schools

SILO	Schools Industry Liaison Officer
SLD	Severe Learning Difficulties
SMP	School Mathematics Project
SOED	Scottish Office Education Department (now renamed: see SOEID)
SOEID	Scottish Office Education and Industry Department
SQA	Scottish Qualifications Authority
SSA	Standard Spending Assessment
SSTA	Scottish Secondary Teachers Association
SVQ	Scottish Vocational Qualification
SWAP	Scottish Wider Access Programme
TEC	Training and Enterprise Council
TEFL	Teaching English as a Foreign Language
TES	*Times Education Supplement*
TESL	Teaching English as a Second Language
TESOL	Teaching of English to Speakers of Other Languages
TGAT	Task Group on Assessment and Testing
THES	*Times Higher Education Supplement*
TPS	Teacher Placement Service
TQA	Teaching Quality Assessment
TTA	Teacher Training Agency
UCAS	Universities and Colleges Admissions Services
UNESCO	United Nations Educational, Scientific and Cultural Organisation
VC	Vice Chancellor
WEA	Workers' Educational Association
WISE	Women into Science and Engineering

SOURCES AND FURTHER READING

A much more comprehensive listing (with over 3,000 entries) will be found in the booklet below and any subsequent editions.

Hutchins, J. (ed.) (1991) *Acronyms and Initialisms in Education: a handlist*, fifth edition, Norwich: Librarians of Institutes and Schools of Education.